GUIDE TO
FINANCIAL AIDS
FOR STUDENTS
IN ARTS & SCIENCES
For Graduate and
Professional Stud

GUIDE TO FINANCIAL AIDS FOR STUDENTS IN ARTS & SCIENCES

For Graduate and Professional Study

First Edition, **AYSEL SEARLES, JR.**

Revised Edition, **ANNE SCOTT**
Assistant Director
Office of Career Plans & Placement
SUNY-Binghamton

arco

New York

Published by Arco Publishing Company, Inc.
219 Park Avenue South, New York, N.Y. 10003

Copyright © 1974, 1971 by Aysel Searles, Jr.

Library of Congress Catalog Card Number 74-80776
ISBN 0-668-02496-8

Printed in the United States of America

funded from an outside source such as a business, foundations, alumni, professional societies or a unit of government.

4. <u>Teaching</u> <u>or</u> <u>research</u> <u>assistantships</u> requiring appropriate services, available only on competitive application directly to the schools, colleges or universities. Such training or research assistantships may be funded by the educational institution to attract competent graduate students, and the stipends may include waiver of tuition. Services of the teaching or research assistant are often utilized in such a way that they are a part of the education of the student. However, full-time graduate course loads are usually not possible under this arrangement.

5. <u>Traineeships</u> requiring appropriate services available only on competitive application directly to the school, college or university. These are usually funded by the federal government in connection with a grant made to a university for a specific research project. Stipends are typically graduated over the period needed to complete the advanced degree and usually include a waiver of tuition and dependency allowances.

6. <u>Work</u> <u>study</u> <u>positions</u>, an increasing form of financial aid. These may be funded by the school, college or university or by Federal funds administered through the institution. Within this category are also resident internships, library aids, student internships in external fields of education or community service, etc.

7. <u>Subsidies</u> in various forms, granted directly or indirectly by state governments or consortia, usually toward or in lieu of tuition and fees. No service is typically required of the student. Another type of subsidy is for veterans in the form of Federal assistance in monthly stipends, state subsidies or competitive scholarships, etc.

8. <u>Loan funds</u>, considered by many students as a last resort in financing graduate or professional education, are available from many sources. Prominent among these sources are the National Direct Student Loan Program, State or Federal Guaranteed Loan programs, United Student Aid Funds and various university loan funds. In most instances, information about such loans is obtainable through the financial aid office of the school, college or university that the candidate plans to attend.

Many scholarships and fellowships carry considerable prestige, in addition to the advantage of not requiring specific services of the successful applicant. They consequently engender a high level of competition, and the potential applicant should present a strong academic record, test scores and/or other special qualifications. Within this rubric, applicants should become familiar with specific requirements well in advance of the probable deadline for applications.

The various types of teaching and research assistantships, trainee-ships and work/study assignments are also often competitive and usually require relatively early application. Even though services are required, these various assistantships are <u>numerous</u> and valuable in terms of money and experience.

The prudent applicant will ascertain well in advance the required information concerning <u>all</u> types of financial aid listed above, and pay careful attention to deadlines, tests and other requirements for such multiple applications as seem indicated in individual circumstances.

Early and numerous applications are recommended. It is better to apply when in doubt, and withdraw later, if necessary. Quantitative estimates regarding grades needed for acceptance are not usually available and could be misleading because of other factors such as test scores, faculty recommendations, etc. There is an increasing tendency toward earlier application deadlines, particularly if financial aid is a factor.

In connection with multiple applications, both within and across fields, it should be recognized that multiple applications present some problems to both the candidate and the schools. For the candidate there are such problems as costly application fees, the need to secure many faculty references, the expenditure of time in completing application forms, fees and time for appropriate admission tests, etc. For the admissions committee or appropriate offices of the graduate and professional schools, multiple applications are somewhat of a nightmare as they attempt comparative assessments, knowing full well that much time is being spent on evaluating candidates who will never enroll, and the problem this creates of admitting too many or too few of the best qualified applicants.

In two fields, medicine and law, an attempt is being made to reduce the effort and expense of both the applicants and the schools. The American College Medical Application Service, developed by admissions officers of member institutions of the Association of American Medical Colleges, and the Law School Data Assembly Service, developed by the Law School Admission Council, have made possible the use of a single application and single transcript. These are processed by the respective services and copies sent to participating member schools, who make autonomous decisions. Such services can be helpful, particularly if all member schools participate, and it is possible that this pattern will be adopted by other types of professional schools. It should be noted, however, that this service

resolves only some of the problems of multiple applications, and not the

most frustrating one of over or underadmission by the schools, which can

have a serious effect on qualified applicants who under other circumstances

might have been admitted to one of the schools of their first, second, or

third choice. Despite these obvious disadvantages, most students must

continue to submit multiple applications for admission.

Financial Aid

Fully as complicated as the choice of a graduate or professional school

is the problem of financial aid for the student in Arts and Sciences who has

spent many thousands of dollars in study at the undergraduate level and who

may not have access to personal or family resources sufficient to finance

further education, or who has already borrowed such large sums that further

indebtedness may not be practical.

Financial aid for graduate and professional study, including disser-

tation research, falls into one or more categories as summarized below, but

is more fully described in appropriate sections of this book:

1. Scholarships and fellowships not requiring services, and awarded by

departments and agencies of Federal or state governments, or by foundations,

organizations or professional societies, through competitive direct

application to the donor.

2. Scholarships and fellowships not requiring services, available only

on competitive application directly to schools, colleges or universities,

made available from their endowments or income.

3. Scholarships and fellowships not requiring services, available only

on competitive application directly to schools, colleges or universities   and

This book is dedicated to the late Aysel Searles Jr., former Director of the Office of Career Plans and Placement at the State University of New York at Binghamton.

Acknowledgements of editorial assistance and typing are particularly due Rosanne Mollen, Anne Giesecke and Elaine Searles.

Foreword

"There is increasing concern over the mounting cost of higher education, and for varying ways to meet the problem.

"The central issue is whether, under the benefit theory, the student is the primary beneficiary and hence should pay most of the cost of his or her education, or whether society is the primary beneficiary and should bear most of the cost.

"If the student is regarded as the only beneficiary, his or her ability to pay the cost of higher education is a problem, which some would seek to resolve by establishing a national student loan bank from which any student could borrow as much as needed for any educational purpose, and subsequently repay out of future earnings. Also at issue are such factors as length of time for repayment, the possibility of interest subsidy, and important questions of the effect of such plans on educational philosophy and curriculum.

"Those who support the position that society is the ultimate benefactor of higher education and should bear most of the cost are divided on what portions should be borne by endowments, gifts and grants from private resources, state governments, and the Federal government. The method of support, whether it be in terms of restricted grants, general institutional aid, direct grants to students, tax rebates to parents, etc., is an issue further complicated because colleges are currently aided in varying degrees by private endowment, religious groups and state funds. Educators are concerned that restricted grants tend to reduce autonomy, curricular diversity and directions of research and public service.

"While much of the discussion about who should finance higher education has focused on the undergraduate level, whatever solutions evolve will have direct bearing on the person considering graduate study. If a significant emphasis is placed on student loans for those unable to meet undergraduate costs, it would appear that society, by one means or another, _must_ undertake the financing of graduate education."

The above message was written by Aysel Searles, Jr. for the first edition of this book. It is maintained in toto for the revised edition as a pertinent reminder that the concern over who should pay the cost of education has not, and most likely will not, be easily resolved. The costs of education are mounting while the amount of financial aid available is decreasing. It is apparent that an increasing emphasis is being placed on loans in various forms thereby putting the burden of repayment on the student. Individuals who choose to attend graduate school only because they "don't know what else to do" may find it difficult to accept this burden. On the other hand, those who have made career decisions that show a need for advanced study and/or specialization will be better prepared to meet the challenge of financing their education.

Anne M. Scott

Contents

Introduction

This book is designed for juniors, seniors and graduate students in the Arts and Sciences who plan any type of additional formal education.

While its focus is on the major resources of financial aid, sections of the Introduction, and the format of entries by broad fields, make it a useful resource as a "career guide" for the undecided person who has not yet made a firm educational/vocational commitment, or who has been turned aside from an objective and is seeking alternatives.

EXCLUDED from consideration in this book are the following:

1. post-doctoral funds;

2. awards to persons already in professional schools or practicing a profession;

3. awards where the total number appears to be less than ten per year;

4. prizes;

5. funds for foreign students, faculty and mature scholars;

6. specific aid for specific schools or universities, with rare exceptions.

The awards described are drawn from material provided by donors and are divided into seven areas (see Table of Contents). An annotated bibliography, rather than being an appendix, is integrated into appropriate areas. The descriptions of the awards are brief and are prefixed by the code letter of the category and numbered within these categories. While this publication has been carefully compiled within the limitations set forth above, it cannot be all-inclusive, and the student should always consult with faculty advisors about other resources.

Application for Advanced Study

Graduate or professional study leading to one or more degrees beyond the baccalaureate is increasingly necessary for students enrolled in programs within the Arts and Sciences.

For most bachelor's degree candidates, the most realistic approach is full-time study in a graduate or professional school. If this is not possible, then plans should be made for summer or part-time study. About half of the degree candidates in colleges of arts and sciences have a goal in mind by the end of their junior year. For this group it is not so much a matter of planning, but rather utilizing the best technique to implement plans. For the undecided there is the additional burden of attempting to analyze one's interests and aptitudes as they may relate to various possible types of graduate or professional study, and the kinds of employment toward which they tend to lead.

The student who is uncertain of his or her professional goals should talk with friends, classmates, faculty and staff advisors, members of various professions, etc. and should read publications concerning multiple or specific career opportunities. Career, by definition, is "an occupation or profession followed as one's life work." For many persons, however, this definition does not suffice. For example, a career in law requires professional training. Subsequently, however, there are many fields of legal work that offer diversity. The lawyer may begin his own practice, or join a law firm, or become the salaried employee of a single client. Some attorneys specialize in areas such as criminal law, tax law or civil rights. Many serve as lawyers for governmental agencies. Political office or the judiciary are frequent objectives of lawyers.

Frequently, persons trained in one profession may assume positions of

responsibility in an unrelated area, hence the term "career planning" must
be viewed by the undecided college student more realistically as the
question, "What type of graduate or professional training seems best for my
present situation?" rather than as an effort to determine a lifetime
occupation.

To assist the undecided student in Arts and Sciences to define some
educational objectives, and to obtain preliminary information about where
such programs are available, major resources include: National Trade and
Professional Associations of the United States (G-5), (Peterson's) Annual
Guides to Graduate Study (G-15) and Occupational Outlook Handbook (G-29).

Use of the publications listed above is recommended for students who
have any uncertainty about their postgraduate plans.

Frequently, in many areas of graduate or professional study, there are
specialized publications concerning educational opportunities in a particular
field or specialization. Such material is usually available within the
appropriate academic department, the university library, or the college
career plans library.

In utilizing these sources to research programs, and where they are
given, the interested student will frequently compile a substantial list of
possible programs and universities. Factors such as geography, cost, size
of the school, etc., may rule out some of these preliminary listings.

Depending upon (1) the number of schools offering the program, (2) the
person's probable strength as a candidate for admission, and (3) the
potential for financial aid, if needed, the candidate should, as soon as
feasible, write each school for a catalog, application and application for
financial aid. He should also give thought as to whom he is planning to
ask for references.

A Study Abroad

A-1   ROME PRIZE FELLOWSHIPS

AMERICAN ACADEMY IN ROME
101 PARK AVENUE
NEW YORK, NEW YORK   10017

Young artists and scholars, men and women of outstanding ability, ready to do independent work in musical composition, painting, sculpture, history of art, architecture, landscape architecture, environmental design, classical studies, and post-classical humanistic studies in Rome may apply for a limited number of fellowships, valued at about $4,600 plus residence and use of Academy facilities. In requesting application forms, state particular field of interest.

Typical Deadline: December 31

A-2   AWARDS OF THE AMERICAN INSTITUTE OF INDIAN STUDIES

AMERICAN INSTITUTE OF INDIAN STUDIES
UNIVERSITY OF CHICAGO
1130 E. 59th STREET
CHICAGO, ILLINOIS   60637

The Institute is a cooperative nonprofit organization whose members are American colleges and universities with a special interest in Indian studies. In addition to awards to established scholars in Indian studies, faculty training and library service fellowships, there are junior fellowships to study in India awarded to graduate students specializing in the Indian aspects of some discipline, who have completed all requirements for the doctoral degree except the dissertation. Also awarded are travel grants and language study fellowships for advanced language study in India.

A-3   AMERICAN-SCANDINAVIAN FOUNDATION

THE AMERICAN-SCANDINAVIAN FOUNDATION
127 EAST 73rd STREET
NEW YORK, NEW YORK   10021

The Foundation sponsors and administers a variety of awards for graduate study in the Scandinavian countries. These include the George C. Marshall Memorial Fund Fellowships for study in Denmark, a Scholar Incentive program for study in Sweden, and a number of fellowships tenable in Sweden, Norway, Finland, Iceland and Denmark. Applicants must be under age 40. Deadlines are for completed applications.

Typical Deadline: November 1
December 1

A-4   ARCTIC SCIENCE - RESEARCH GRANTS-IN-AID

            THE ARCTIC INSTITUTE OF NORTH AMERICA
            1619 NEW HAMPSHIRE AVENUE, N.W.
            WASHINGTON, D. C.   20009

    The Arctic Institute has grants-in-aid to qualified investigators
interested in performing field research in problems relating to the Arctic
Ocean and the adjacent land area. Specifically, inquiry is invited to such
disciplines as physical and chemical oceanography, biological oceanography,
cold weather physiology, geophysics, permafrost, portable water supplies,
and pollution. Field facilities are available at the Naval Arctic Research
Laboratory, Barrow, Alaska, and its field stations for logistic support of
approved programs.

A-5   SCHOLARSHIPS GUIDE FOR COMMONWEALTH POSTGRADUATE STUDENTS

            THE ASSOCIATION OF COMMONWEALTH UNIVERSITIES
            36 GORDON SQUARE
            LONDON, WCIH OPF
            ENGLAND

    This publication describes scholarships, grants, assistantships,
etc., open to graduates of Commonwealth universities who wish to undertake
postgraduate (including postdoctoral) study or research at a Commonwealth
university outside their own country. Although the book is aimed primarily
at graduates of Commonwealth universities, very many of the awards listed
are also open to students from the USA contemplating study, research or
teaching in Britain, Australia or Canada. Cost of this 250-page handbook is
six dollars which includes second class air mail postage.

A-6   SCHOLARSHIPS FOR STUDY IN AUSTRIA

            AUSTRIA INSTITUTE
            11 EAST 52nd STREET
            NEW YORK, NEW YORK   10022

    The Austrian government offers a limited number of scholarships for
study at any Austrian institution of higher education during each academic
year. The value is listed at approximately $225 per month for nine months
and is regarded as sufficient for room, board, and tuition for a single
person. Applications should be made to the Institute of International
Education, 809 United Nations Plaza, New York, New York   10017.

                                        Typical Deadline: October 15

-7   BELGIAN-AMERICAN EDUCATIONAL FOUNDATION INCORPORATED

        BELGIAN-AMERICAN EDUCATIONAL FOUNDATION INCORPORATED
        420 LEXINGTON AVENUE
        NEW YORK, NEW YORK   10017

    The purpose of these awards is to allow representative American
scholars to pursue independent study and research in Belgium on projects
for which Belgium provides special advantages. Nominations are made by the
Dean of the Graduate School in which the candidate is studying or teaching.
American citizenship and a speaking and reading knowledge of French or
Flemish are necessary qualifications. In addition, candidates may be
holders of the Ph.D. or equivalent degree, or faculty. Preference is given
to those under 35. The stipend for ten-month tenure is $4,500.

                                    Typical Deadline: January 31

A-8   MARSHALL SCHOLARSHIPS

        BRITISH EMBASSY
        3100 MASSACHUSETTS AVENUE, N.W.
        WASHINGTON, D. C.   20008

    Thirty Marshall Scholarships are offered annually, the awards
being split between five regions of the United States with the remaining
ten chosen at large. Men and women under twenty-six as of October 1 are
eligible and the scholarship is tenable at any university in the United
Kingdom. Selection is based on distinction of intellect and character as
evidenced by scholastic attainment and by other activities and achievements.
The awards are made at approximately $3,800 per academic year for two years,
but may be extended for a third year. In certain circumstances a marriage
allowance is payable.

                                    Typical Deadline: Early October

A-9   STUDY IN BRITAIN

        BRITISH INFORMATION SERVICES
        POLICY AND REFERENCE DIVISION
        845 THIRD AVENUE
        NEW YORK, NEW YORK   10022

    This mimeographed publication describes some scholarship and
exchange opportunities for American students in Britain.

A-10   <u>AWARDS</u> <u>FOR</u> <u>GRADUATE</u> <u>STUDY</u> <u>AND</u> <u>RESEARCH</u> - (CANADA)

        STATISTICS CANADA
        EDUCATION, SCIENCE & CULTURE DIVISION
        STUDENT INFORMATION SECTION
        OTTAWA K1A OZ5, ONTARIO
        CANADA

        This extensive publication is intended primarily for Canadians,
but indication is given as to which of the awards tenable in Canada are
open to students from abroad. It contains about 2,000 entries on awards
available to university graduates from sources in Canada, the United States,
the United Kingdom and several other countries. A revised edition will be
published at about four dollars.

A-11   <u>FELLOWSHIP</u> <u>GUIDE</u> <u>FOR</u> <u>WESTERN</u> <u>EUROPE</u>

        COUNCIL FOR EUROPEAN STUDIES
        156 MERVIS HALL
        UNIVERSITY OF PITTSBURGH
        PITTSBURGH, PENNSYLVANIA   15260

        This 82-page publication is a good resource at all levels of
educational achievement for persons who wish to study in European
universities, primarily in the social sciences and humanities. It is not,
however, a full substitute for <u>Study</u> <u>Abroad</u>, the UNESCO publication, or
<u>Handbook</u> <u>of</u> <u>International</u> <u>Study</u> <u>for</u> <u>U. S.</u> <u>Nationals</u>, published by the
Institute of International Education, or several other publications
mentioned in this Section as well as in Section G. Price: $2.00

A-12   PRE-DISSERTATION TRAINING PROGRAM (EUROPE)

        COUNCIL FOR EUROPEAN STUDIES
        156 MERVIS HALL
        UNIVERSITY OF PITTSBURGH
        PITTSBURGH, PENNSYLVANIA   15260

        This program enables selected graduate students to spend a summer
(or an equivalent period) in Europe, prior to beginning their dissertations,
to acquire field experience and to sharpen skills vital to their research
activities. Further information is available from the address above.

A-13   GERMAN ACADEMIC EXCHANGE SERVICE

DEUTSCHER AKADEMISCHER AUSTAUSCHDIENST
53 BONN - BAD GODESBERG
KENNEDY-ALLEE 50
FEDERAL REPUBLIC OF GERMANY

Scholarships for study in Germany are awarded to graduates and postgraduates of all academic disciplines, as well as music and fine arts. These awards are substantial and cover travel and living costs, tuition, books, family allowance, etc. The grant period is 10 months. Good academic record and good command of the German language are needed. Maximum age 32 years. Deadline for application with the Institute of International Education, 809 United Nations Plaza, New York, New York: November 1. Further details will be furnished by the Fulbright advisors on university campuses or by the German Academic Exchange Service, New York Office, One Fifth Avenue, New York, New York   10003.

A-14   DOHERTY FELLOWSHIPS FOR LATIN AMERICAN STUDIES

DOHERTY FELLOWSHIP COMMITTEE
PROGRAM IN LATIN AMERICAN STUDIES
240 EAST PYNE
PRINCETON, NEW JERSEY   08540

Financed by the Henry L. and Grace Doherty Charitable Foundation, Inc. are a limited number of fellowships for advanced study in Latin America in the field of the social studies. Grants are for graduate students (or advanced scholars) whose primary interest is in Latin American studies and provide full travel and subsistence for one year for the grantee and dependent family, plus support of minimal research needs. Limited to United States citizens.

Typical Deadline: February 1

A-15   EAST-WEST CENTER GRADUATE STUDY GRANTS

          OFFICE OF PARTICIPANT SERVICES
          THE EAST-WEST CENTER
          HONOLULU, HAWAII   96822

     The East-West Center offers graduate study grants for its programs
which seek solutions to some of the major human problems of mutual concern
to the peoples of the United States, Asia and the Pacific. These
all-inclusive grants provide for graduate study in the University of Hawaii
and directed research, training and field education through East-West
Center Institutes. These Institutes are concerned with communications,
language and culture, food, population, and the effects of technology.
Instruction in an Asian/Pacific language is required and research may be
undertaken in Asia and the Pacific area.

                                            Typical Deadline: December 15

A-16   FOREIGN AREA FELLOWSHIPS FOR AFRICA AND THE NEAR EAST
          (ADVANCED GRADUATE)

          SOCIAL SCIENCE RESEARCH COUNCIL
          110 EAST 59th STREET
          NEW YORK, NEW YORK   10022

     Fellowships are available for graduate training or research abroad
related to Africa or the Near and Middle East. The program offers limited
opportunities for preparatory training directly related to a research
proposal, in the United States or Canada, but is designed primarily to
support field research by qualified pre-doctoral students who have completed
all requirements for the Ph.D. except the dissertation. Students with
appropriate professional degrees (i.e., urban planning) may also apply.
Fellowships are customarily for 12 months. Stipends for study in the
United States range upward from $250 per month. Research abroad is
supported with a living stipend, transportation, allowances for dependents
and a limited research expense allowance.

                                            Typical Deadline: November 10

A-17   FOREIGN AREA FELLOWSHIPS PROGRAM AWARDS FOR DOCTORAL DISSERTATION
        RESEARCH IN LATIN AMERICA AND THE CARIBBEAN

        SOCIAL SCIENCE RESEARCH COUNCIL
        110 EAST 59th STREET
        NEW YORK, NEW YORK   10022

An applicant need not be a Latin American or Caribbean specialist, but must be trained in a discipline which may be applied to the study of development in the area. Language competence must be such as to carry out the proposed programs. Applicants must have completed all Ph.D. requirements except the dissertation. Research awards will be in association with universities or other organizations. Awards are for up to 24 months and cover basic maintenance and travel, including dependents. Additional support may come from the institution of affiliation.

                                        Typical Deadline: November 30

A-18   FELLOWSHIPS AND GRANTS FOR TRAINING AND RESEARCH ON FOREIGN AREAS

        SOCIAL SCIENCE RESEARCH COUNCIL
        230 PARK AVENUE
        NEW YORK, NEW YORK   10017

Entries A-16, A-17 and A-19 are examples of fellowships cosponsored by the Social Science Research Council and the American Council of Learned Societies. In general, the fellowships are offered to support doctoral dissertation research abroad in the humanities and social sciences. Stipends normally include maintenance and transportation, a research allowance, health insurance and limited assistance toward tuition costs. In addition to the areas in A-16, A-17 and A-19, fellowship programs are offered for: East, Southeast and South Asia, Near and Middle East, Contemporary and Republican China, East Europe, Japan and Korea. Further information concerning program purposes, eligibility requirement and application deadlines can be obtained from the above address.

A-19   FELLOWSHIPS FOR WESTERN EUROPE

          SOCIAL SCIENCE RESEARCH COUNCIL
          WESTERN EUROPEAN FELLOWSHIP PROGRAM
          110 EAST 59th STREET
          NEW YORK, NEW YORK   10022

     Fellowships are offered to citizens of permanent residents of the
United States and Canada, enrolled in full-time graduate studies in a North
American institution, for doctoral dissertation research in Western Europe.
Particular emphasis is given to students in disciplines which have devoted
relatively less attention to Western Europe, such as economics, sociology,
anthropology and social psychology, though applications are accepted from
students in all social sciences and the humanities. The fellowships support
field research in Western Europe, plus occasional preliminary training.
Fellowships include maintenance stipend, travel and a small research
allowance.

                                        Typical Deadline: November 30

A-20   FULBRIGHT-HAYS PROGRAMS (GENERAL DESCRIPTION)

     The administration of the various Fulbright-Hays Awards, one of
the largest programs to subsidize study, teaching and research abroad,
appears somewhat complex as five groups are involved in various parts of
the total aid program. The Board of Foreign Scholarships is responsible for
making policy, and its 12 members are appointed by the President of the
United States. The Department of State, through its bureau of Educational
and Cultural Affairs, has prime responsibility for administration of that
policy, both here and abroad. To supervise the day-to-day operations of the
program, the State Department contracts for the services of three agencies.

     The Institute of International Education supervises foreign students
who have grants to study in the United States. It is also under contract to
the State Department to organize publicity, receive and process applications
and make recommendations for graduate study grants. Separately, the
Institute of International Education, under agreements with foreign
governments, universities, and private donors, performs the same functions
with regard to grants sponsored by them.

     The Conference Board of Associated Research Councils cooperates
with the Department of State in the exchange of lecturers and research
scholars, primarily at the college and university level.

     The Office of Education Institute of International Studies, in a
working fund arrangement with the Department of State, cooperates in
exchange of teachers primarily at the elementary and secondary level,
including summer seminar study abroad, and simultaneously arranges the
programs for foreign teachers visiting the United States. In addition,
the Institute of International Studies administers the Foreign Area and

Language Training Program, designed to promote and improve modern foreign language training and area studies in American education. In addition to institutional grants and grants to foreign curriculum specialists, this branch of the Department of Health, Education and Welfare provides grants for teachers and prospective teachers at all levels to do research and study abroad in the field of foreign languages and area studies. Also, they administer Graduate Fellowships for dissertation research, study/research, and higher education faculty programs for curriculum development, for curriculum specialists in foreign language and area studies at all levels, and in all areas of education. Each campus usually has a "Fulbright" advisor.

A-21   ALLIANCE FRANCAISE DE NEW YORK SCHOLARSHIPS

        INFORMATION AND REFERENCE DIVISION
        INSTITUTE OF INTERNATIONAL EDUCATION
        809 UNITED NATIONS PLAZA
        NEW YORK, NEW YORK   10017

        Scholarships are offered on behalf of Alliance Francaise by I.I.E. in conjunction with the Fulbright-Hays grants. Applications will be considered from well-qualified students in all academic fields for graduate study in France. French and American nationals are eligible and must be between twenty and thirty years of age. For Americans, proficiency in written and spoken French is necessary. Each scholarship is in the amount of $1,100 per annum and is for a period of one year. Initial information may be obtained from the Campus Fulbright Program Advisor, or the address above.

                                Typical Deadline: November 1

A-22   FRENCH GOVERNMENT GRANTS

        INSTITUTE OF INTERNATIONAL EDUCATION
        809 UNITED NATIONS PLAZA
        NEW YORK, NEW YORK   10017

        The French government offers grants and assistantships to American graduate students. All information and applications are to be obtained from the Institute at the address above, or from the Fulbright Program advisor on campus.

                                Typical Deadline: November 1

A-23   FULBRIGHT-HAYS AND OTHER AWARDS FOR STUDY ABROAD - PRE-DOCTORAL

> INSTITUTE OF INTERNATIONAL EDUCATION
> 809 UNITED NATIONS PLAZA
> NEW YORK, NEW YORK   10017

The Institute coordinates and administers an assortment of financial aids, and is a prime contact for fellowships and grants to study abroad. Applications are accepted from May 1 to November 1 of the year preceding the award. The Institute helps administer many United States grants, such as portions of the Fulbright-Hays Act, under contract with the State Department, as well as foreign grants on behalf of other governments, universities and private donors. Described in their publication, Grants for Graduate Study Abroad, are: Fulbright-Hays Full Grants, Fulbright-Hays Travel Grants, Foreign Grants and Special Programs which include direct exchanges and opportunities for recent graduates and M.A. candidates as well as teaching opportunities. Information may be obtained from your campus Fulbright Program Advisor or from the above address.

A-24   EXCHANGE PROGRAMS WITH EASTERN EUROPE AND THE SOVIET UNION

> INTERNATIONAL RESEARCH AND EXCHANGES BOARD
> 110 EAST 59th STREET
> NEW YORK, NEW YORK   10022

Established in 1968 by the American Council of Learned Societies and the Social Science Research Council, IREX administers academic exchange programs between scholars in the United States and the countries of East-Central and Southeast Europe and the Soviet Union. Programs are available in Bulgaria, Czechoslovakia, Hungary, Poland, Romania and Yugoslavia, as well as in the USSR.

Participants in the regular exchange programs are placed at appropriate institutions of higher learning in the host country, where they undertake individual research projects for periods of two to ten months. Candidates must be faculty members or advanced doctoral candidates who will have completed all requirements for the Ph.D. except the thesis by the time of participation. They are expected to have mastery of the language of the host country sufficient for the purposes of their research and study. Deadlines for these exchanges are in November and December.

IREX also administers a summer language program in the Soviet Union for teachers of the Russian language, and several peripheral grant programs. These include the ad hoc grants to promote new exchanges--a limited number of grants given to individuals and institutions wishing to arrange new forms of scholarly contact and exchange are considered quarterly, with deadlines on September 30, December 31, March 30 and June 30. A small number of grants are also given for collaborative projects in the social sciences or humanities involving scholars from the U. S. and one or more of the exchange countries.

Typical Deadlines: October 31
April 30

A-25   THE NETHERLAND-AMERICA FOUNDATION

THE NETHERLAND-AMERICA FOUNDATION, INCORPORATED
ONE ROCKEFELLER PLAZA
NEW YORK, NEW YORK   10020

Americans who wish to study in Holland are offered loans based on need, worthiness and willingness to repay. Outright grants of $300 to $500 are usually given competitively and to supplement a grant from another source. Both loans and grants are limited to those who will "build friendship and understanding between the two nations."

Typical Deadline: March 1

A-26   ORGANIZATION OF AMERICAN STATES

OFFICE OF FELLOWSHIPS AND TRAINING
SECRETARIAT FOR TECHNICAL COOPERATION
ORGANIZATION OF AMERICAN STATES
WASHINGTON, D.C.   20006

Fellowships are tenable in member countries of the OAS and are for advanced study or research. Detailed plans are required for either type of grant, and language proficiency is necessary. Fellowships may range from three months to two years and may include travel expenses, tuition, fees and room and board. Among the fields open to United States citizens are Latin American area studies, language and linguistic studies, economic problems of any social science discipline, Latin American law and legal systems, anthropological and archeological studies, library science, etc.

Typical Deadlines: December 31
June 30

A-27   THE RHODES SCHOLARSHIPS

> THE RHODES SCHOLARSHIP OFFICE
> WESLEYAN UNIVERSITY
> MIDDLETOWN, CONNECTICUT   06457

Thirty-two scholarships are available for two or possibly three years of study at the University of Oxford. Candidates must be unmarried males, between 18 and 24 years of age, and by the time of application must have at least Junior standing. The scholarships are assigned to eight district groupings of states where final selection results in four grantees per district. The stipend pays all tuition and fees at a college of the University of Oxford, and an ample maintenance allowance. In addition to literary and scholastic attainments, selection committees consider "character, and fondness for, and success in sports." Financial need, race or religious opinion are not factors.

Typical Deadline: October

A-28   ROTARY FOUNDATION AWARDS FOR INTERNATIONAL UNDERSTANDING

> ROTARY INTERNATIONAL
> 1600 RIDGE AVENUE
> EVANSTON, ILLINOIS   60201

In addition to undergraduate scholarships and technical training awards, the Rotary Foundation offers graduate fellowships for an academic year of study abroad with expenses paid. In addition to his or her program of studies, the grantee is expected to act as "an ambassador of goodwill." In the absence of language proficiency in "non-Western" languages, the Foundation will also pay expenses for up to three months of language study. The awards are tenable in any of the 149 countries or territories in which there are Rotary Clubs. Applications are made through the Rotary Club district in which the applicant resides, or is presently studying, and forms are available one and one half years preceding the planned study.

A-29   STUDY ABROAD

> UNITED NATIONS EDUCATIONAL, SCIENTIFIC AND CULTURAL ORGANIZATION
> 7 PLACE FONTENOY
> PARIS, FRANCE

The scholarships and fellowships listed in Volume XIX of Study Abroad are indexed by chapters according to the donors or awards as follows: International Organizations printed in English, French and Spanish; and by states and territories in alphabetical order according to the country in which the donor is located. Countries are listed in one language only according to the national language, or that normally used for official communications. Offers are listed according to coded fields of study. In general, applications are to be directed to the donor anywhere from 6 to 12 months before the beginning of the applicable academic year. This publication is available for six dollars plus postage from UNIPUB, Box 433, New York, New York 10016.

A-30   FULBRIGHT-HAYS DOCTORAL DISSERTATION RESEARCH ABROAD FELLOWSHIPS

DIVISION OF FOREIGN STUDIES
INSTITUTE OF INTERNATIONAL STUDIES
OFFICE OF EDUCATION
U.S. DEPARTMENT OF HEALTH, EDUCATION AND WELFARE
WASHINGTON, D. C.   20202

This program enables advanced graduate students to engage in full-time dissertation research abroad in modern foreign languages, area studies and world affairs. Awards are made for 6 to 12 months and fellows must plan to teach in the U.S. at the post-secondary level. Awards are not available for projects focusing on England, France, Germany, Italy or Spain. Candidates must apply through their institutions, present research proposals and possess language skills necessary to carry out the project.

Typical Deadline: October 15

A-31   FULBRIGHT-HAYS ACT - OPPORTUNITIES ABROAD FOR TEACHERS - EDUCATIONAL EXCHANGES

TEACHER EXCHANGE SECTION
DIVISION OF INTERNATIONAL EXCHANGE AND TRAINING
INSTITUTE OF INTERNATIONAL STUDIES
OFFICE OF EDUCATION
U.S. DEPARTMENT OF HEALTH, EDUCATION AND WELFARE
WASHINGTON, D.C.   20202

Elementary and secondary school teachers, college instructors and assistant professors are eligible to participate in the teacher exchange program which offers grants to teach or attend summer seminars abroad. Successful, full-time teaching experience is a prerequisite, and facility in the language of the host country is desirable or necessary. Apply during the period September 1 to November 1 to the Institute of International Studies at the address above.

A

SPECIFIC CROSS REFERENCES

In addition to the references preceding, _every_ candidate for financial aid is urged to read Section G in toto. This section describes financial aid publications, as well as important loan funds and grants which are not restricted to specific areas of graduate or professional study.

B   Arts and Sciences

This section delineates special sources of financial aid for graduate study and dissertation research within the traditional disciplines of the Arts and Sciences.

B-1   GRADUATE FELLOWSHIPS FOR WOMEN (DISSERTATION AWARDS)

AMERICAN ASSOCIATION OF UNIVERSITY WOMEN
EDUCATIONAL FOUNDATION
2401 VIRGINIA AVENUE, N.W.
WASHINGTON, D. C.   20037

Stipends of $2,500 to $5,000 are available to American women who will have fulfilled all requirements for the doctorate except the dissertation by January 2 preceding the fellowship year which is July 1 to June 30. Fifty of these awards are typically granted. The A.A.U.W. applications for the Graduate Fellowships are available August 1, and there are no restrictions as to age or field of study.

Typical Deadline: January 2

B-2   DISSERTATION FELLOWSHIPS, BANKING AND FINANCE, STONIER FELLOWSHIPS

AMERICAN BANKERS ASSOCIATION
EDUCATION COUNCIL
HAROLD STONIER FELLOWSHIP PROGRAM
1120 CONNECTICUT AVENUE, N.W.
WASHINGTON, D. C.   20036

A very limited number of fellowships for dissertation research in banking, finance or economics is offered, with the stipend of $3,500 for one academic year, plus tuition and fees.

Typical Deadline: March 1

B-3   FELLOWSHIPS IN LEGAL HISTORY (DOCTORAL DISSERTATION)

            PROJECT IN LEGAL HISTORY
            AMERICAN BAR FOUNDATION
            1155 EAST 60th STREET
            CHICAGO, ILLINOIS   60637

    In addition to awards to persons holding a law or doctoral degree,
the American Bar Foundation will offer three- to twelve-month fellowships to
a few persons who have passed the qualifying examinations for the Ph.D. in
history or a related subject and who have begun research for the doctoral
dissertation. The awards are to assist scholars engaged in legal historical
studies to bring to fruition original research in Anglo-American legal
history. No period is excluded, but principal concern is with the period
1500-1800 in Anglo-American legal history and 1800-1900 in American legal
history.

                                        Typical Deadline: February 1

B-4   AMERICAN COUNCIL OF LEARNED SOCIETIES

            AMERICAN COUNCIL OF LEARNED SOCIETIES
            345 EAST 46th STREET
            NEW YORK, NEW YORK   10017

    "The Council is a federation of national organizations concerned
with the humanities--the languages and literatures, philosophies and
religious, history and the arts, and the associated techniques--and the
humanistic elements in the social sciences." The ACLS administers grants
primarily on the post-doctoral level; however, graduate students who have
completed at least one year of graduate study, and who have a commitment
to advanced study in the humanities and social sciences may apply under the
East European Language Program. This summer abroad program provides grants
for study of the languages of Albania, Bulgaria, Czechoslovakia, Greece,
Hungary, Poland, Romania and Yugoslavia. For additional information,
contact the academic department or the ACLS.

                                         Typical Deadline: February 1

<u>NOTICES</u> <u>OF</u> <u>THE</u> <u>AMERICAN</u> <u>MATHEMATICAL</u> <u>SOCIETY</u> - SPECIAL ISSUE

         AMERICAN MATHEMATICAL SOCIETY
         321 SOUTH MAIN STREET
         P.O. BOX 6248
         PROVIDENCE, RHODE ISLAND   02904

     The 12th annual Special Issue of the <u>Notices</u> contains a list of
assistantships and fellowships in mathematics, a selected list of stipends,
articles on tax status of grants and an index of abstracts. The list of
assistantships and fellowships available for 1973-74 includes 481 departments
of mathematics, statistics, computer science and related mathematical
disciplines representing 345 universities and colleges. The December 1972
Special Issue, Volume 19, Number 8, costs three dollars. There is an annual
revision.

B-6   THE THEODORE ROOSEVELT MEMORIAL FUND (WILDLIFE CONSERVATION -
        NATURAL HISTORY)

         AMERICAN MUSEUM OF NATURAL HISTORY
         CENTRAL PARK WEST AT 79th STREET
         NEW YORK, NEW YORK   10024

     The grants will be made to younger scientists, in particular
graduate students, and are designed to assist individuals conducting research
in all phases of wildlife conservation or related fields of North American
natural history, with particular reference to North American fauna. Grants
may be obtained for travel and living expenses at any location in North
America (north of Mexico) and may cover trips to New York City to study the
Museum's collections, or for work at any of the Museum's field stations.

                                        Typical Deadline: March 1

B-7   GRANTS FOR SUMMER STUDY IN NUMISMATICS

         THE AMERICAN NUMISMATIC SOCIETY
         BROADWAY AND 155th STREET
         NEW YORK, NEW YORK   10032

     Ten grants-in-aid for study at the Society's museum have been
offered to students of high competence who completed at least one year of
graduate study in classics, archeology, Oriental studies, history, art
history or other humanistic fields. Junior faculty may also apply. A
nine-week program of seminars, lectures and conferences is arranged; and
the grants are $600 each.

                                        Typical Deadline: March 1

B-8   CONGRESSIONAL FELLOWSHIP PROGRAM (WORK-RESEARCH)

          THE AMERICAN POLITICAL SCIENCE ASSOCIATION
          1527 NEW HAMPSHIRE AVENUE, N.W.
          WASHINGTON, D. C.   20036

     Political Scientists who are completing or are near completion of
the Ph.D. and who are teaching or intend to teach, may apply for these
Congressional Fellowships. Involved is a one-month orientation period plus
eight months working as a full-time aid to members of the House and Senate,
or on the staff of a Congressional Committee. There should be an
opportunity for research. Journalists and law school faculty members are
also eligible. The minimum award is $6,500.

                                        Typical Deadline: December 1

B-9   GRADUATE STUDY IN PSYCHOLOGY

          EDUCATIONAL AFFAIRS OFFICE
          AMERICAN PSYCHOLOGICAL ASSOCIATION
          1200 SEVENTEENTH STREET, N.W.
          WASHINGTON, D. C.   20036

     This annual publication gives detailed information on how to apply
to graduate school, admission requirements, government stipends, military
training programs, financial aids and programs of departments of
psychology in the United States and Canada. Available at the address above.

B-10   AMERICAN STUDIES, FINANCIAL AID TO GRADUATE STUDENTS

          AMERICAN QUARTERLY
          AMERICAN STUDIES ASSOCIATION
          BOX 30
          BENNETT HALL
          UNIVERSITY OF PENNSYLVANIA
          PHILADELPHIA, PENNSYLVANIA   19104

     The American Studies Association publishes annually in the summer
supplement issue of American Quarterly information on financial aid
currently available to graduate students of American civilization. Most of
this information is a listing of fellowships and assistantships being
offered by universities with programs in American studies.

B-11   INTERNATIONAL PHYSICS AND ASTRONOMY DIRECTORY

> W.A. BENJAMIN, INCORPORATED
> ADVANCED BOOK PROGRAM
> READING, MASSACHUSETTS   01867

This book lists academic departments and faculties in physics and astronomy and has a faculty index, a geographical index, a list of laboratories, societies, meetings of organizations, grants and fellowships, research in science education, journals, books in print and a directory of publishers. This is a good example of similar books published by field of interest, more commonly by the professional association in the specific field. No attempt is made to list many similar books and journals as it is assumed that departmental offices, as well as libraries, will have such publications available to interested students.

B-12   CAREER ADVANCEMENT SCHOLARSHIPS (WOMEN ONLY)

> BUSINESS AND PROFESSIONAL WOMEN'S FOUNDATION
> 2012 MASSACHUSETTS AVENUE, N.W.
> WASHINGTON, D. C.   20036

These awards are for part-time or full-time study which will assist mature women who need further education or training in order to enter a career field or to improve their chances for professional advancement.

Typical Deadline: Quarterly

B-13   LENA LAKE FORREST FELLOWSHIP FUND (DOCTORAL CANDIDATE RESEARCH)

> BUSINESS AND PROFESSIONAL WOMEN'S FOUNDATION
> 2012 MASSACHUSETTS AVENUE, N.W.
> WASHINGTON, D. C.   20036

The proposed research must pertain to educational, economic, political, social or psychological factors affecting the business and professional woman. Fellowships are awarded to doctoral candidates and range from $500 to $3,000 for one year.

Typical Deadline: January 1

B-14   DANFORTH FELLOWSHIPS

          THE DANFORTH FOUNDATION
          222 SOUTH CENTRAL AVENUE
          ST. LOUIS, MISSOURI   63105

        Danforth Fellowships offer personal encouragement and financial
support to selected college seniors and recent graduates who seek to become
college teachers, and who are vitally interested in relating their
educational plans to their basic values. In selecting Danforth Fellows,
special attention is given to three areas: 1. Evidence of intellectual
ability which is flexible and of wide range; of academic achievement which
is a thorough foundation for graduate study. 2. Evidence of personal
characteristics which are likely to contribute to effective teaching and to
constructive relationships with students. 3. Evidence of a concern for the
relation of ethical or religious values to disciplines, the educational
process and to academic and social responsibility. Applicants must be
under 35 years of age at the time application papers are filed, and may not
have undertaken any graduate or professional study beyond the baccalaureate.
Candidates for appointment are restricted to those persons nominated by
liaison officers (faculty members appointed by college presidents) in
accredited undergraduate colleges in the United States.

                                        Typical Deadline: November 1

B-15   KENT FELLOWSHIPS

          THE DANFORTH FOUNDATION
          222 SOUTH CENTRAL AVENUE
          ST. LOUIS, MISSOURI   63105

        The Fellowships offer encouragement and financial support for the
completion of the doctorate to persons preparing for college teaching. A
minimum of one year of full-time graduate study applicable toward a Ph.D.
in any field of study common to the undergraduate liberal arts curriculum
in the U.S. must be completed and applicants must be less than thirty-five
years of age at the time of application. Candidates are required to have
endorsement from a member of their graduate department. Endorsement forms
are available from the Foundation beginning September 15 and completed
endorsements are due by December 15; completed applications by December 31.

B-16   BYZANTINE STUDIES DISSERTATION FELLOWSHIPS

        DUMBARTON OAKS CENTER FOR BYZANTINE STUDIES
        1703 THIRTY-SECOND STREET, N.W.
        WASHINGTON, D. C.   20007

A limited number of Junior Fellowships are offered to qualified
students of history, archeology, history of art, philology, theology and
other disciplines who wish to write their doctoral dissertations about an
aspect of the Byzantine civilization. A working knowledge of Latin, and in
most cases, ancient Greek is necessary. The stipends are $4,000 for single
and $4,500 for married Fellows in addition to furnished accommodations.

                                Typical Deadline: January 1

B-17   THE GRADUATE RECORD EXAMINATION

        EDUCATIONAL TESTING SERVICE
        BOX 955
        PRINCETON, NEW JERSEY   08540
                or
        BOX 1502
        BERKELEY, CALIFORNIA   94701

For those interested in graduate study, and many state and national
fellowships in the Arts and Sciences, the test most often required is The
Graduate Record Examination. This test is designed primarily for seniors
or upper juniors, and the morning program is a general aptitude examination
yielding a verbal and a quantitative score. The afternoon tests are subject
oriented, and currently offered are "Advanced Tests" in 19 subjects. The
current fee is ten dollars for the Aptitude (morning) Test, and ten dollars
for the Advanced (afternoon) Test. Reports are sent without charge to three
institutions and subsequent reports are two dollars each. Scores are
released only upon request of the candidate. It is possible to take the
test and have scores sent only to you.

        These examinations are usually given in October, December, January,
February, April and July, and are given at most colleges. The October
or December tests are often the dates required for fellowships.

        Current information and applications are available from the nearest
college or university or from an office of Educational Testing Service.

B-18   GRADUATE SCHOOL FOREIGN LANGUAGE TESTS

         GRADUATE SCHOOL FOREIGN LANGUAGE TESTS
         EDUCATIONAL TESTING SERVICE
         BOX 519
         PRINCETON, NEW JERSEY   08540

     This relatively new test is required by some graduate and pro-
fessional schools to meet foreign language reading requirements for
advanced degrees. The GSFLT measures ability to read and understand
professional literature written in French, German, Russian or Spanish.
This test should not be confused with the advanced test in languages of
the Graduate Record Examination, and registration for GSFLT should be made
only if it is a requirement of the graduate or professional school you plan
to attend. Students should consult the graduate chairman of their
departments or their faculty advisor to determine whether their department
uses the GSFLT to determine foreign language reading proficiency.

B-19   THE UNIVERSITY CONSORTIUM FOR WORLD ORDER STUDIES

         THE UNIVERSITY CONSORTIUM FOR WORLD ORDER STUDIES
         FELLOWSHIP PROGRAM
         1855 BROADWAY - 12th FLOOR
         NEW YORK, NEW YORK   10023

     The University Consortium for World Order Studies comprises scholars
at six major universities interested in advancing research on topics
affecting international peace and justice. Among their joint programs is a
graduate-level fellowship program designed to support doctoral dissertation
research and post-doctoral research projects on topics in international law
and organization, transnational economics and social movements, global
environmental issues, arms control and conflict resolution and similar
topics. The fellowships are awarded for periods of work from three months
to one year, with the possibility of renewal. The awards vary in amount
according to the needs and resources of the applicant. The fellowships are
awarded only for study at or under the auspices of one of the six Consortium
institutions: Harvard, Yale, Princeton and Columbia Universities; the
University of California at Berkeley; and the Massachusetts Institute of
Technology. The closing date for applications is February 1 for awards for
the following academic year. About thirty fellowships are awarded each year.

B-20   DISSERTATION RESEARCH GRANTS - GEOLOGY

THE GEOLOGICAL SOCIETY OF AMERICA
3300 PENROSE PLACE
BOULDER, COLORADO   80301

The Society will accept research proposals at the doctoral level for grants within the rubric of "the promotion of the science of Geology," particularly for the promising Ph.D. candidate to do worthwhile field or laboratory work. In general, grants can be used for travel, subsistence materials and supplies directly related to the fulfillment of the research contract.

Typical Deadline: February 15

B-21   GRAPHIC COMMUNICATIONS FELLOWSHIPS

EDUCATION COUNCIL OF THE GRAPHIC ARTS INDUSTRY
GRAPHIC ARTS TECHNICAL CENTER
4615 FORBES AVENUE
PITTSBURGH, PENNSYLVANIA   15213

A number of fellowships for graduate study are available for college graduates who want to pursue advanced training in some specialized area of graphic communications -- printing, publishing, packaging and allied industries.

Typical Deadline: February 1

B-22   SUMMER FELLOWSHIPS IN PHYSIOLOGY

THE GRASS FOUNDATION
77 RESERVOIR ROAD
QUINCY, MASSACHUSETTS   02170

Students in the predoctoral or early postdoctoral category who are interested in physiological research are eligible for the fellowships for summer study at the Marine Biological Laboratories, Woods Hole, Massachusetts. Travel, laboratory and living expenses plus a modest stipend for personal expenses are provided. Applications are individually prepared following guidelines available from the Foundation.

Typical Deadline: January 1

B-23   HAGLEY MUSEUM PROGRAM

>   HAGLEY PROGRAM
>   ELEUTHERIAN MILLS - HAGLEY FOUNDATION
>   GREENVILLE
>   WILMINGTON, DELAWARE   19807

The Foundation and the University of Delaware jointly sponsor a program of graduate study leading to a Master of Arts and/or Doctor of Philosophy degree in United States history for students who plan careers as college teachers or researchers in business, economic or technological history or who plan careers as administrators of historical agencies such as museums, historical societies, libraries and restorations. The first year stipend is $225 per month; second, third and fourth year students receive $250 per month. In addition, all tuition fees are paid by the foundation and there is a $100 per month allowance for married students with dependent children and $300 travel and research allowance for each student. Hagley Fellows supported by the National Endowment for the Humanities receive $200 per month on a twelve-month basis, plus tuition and $500 travel and research allowance.

Typical Deadline: March 1

B-24   HUGHES DOCTORAL FELLOWSHIPS (SCIENCE, MATHEMATICS   AND
         ENGINEERING)

>   HUGHES AIRCRAFT COMPANY
>   SCIENTIFIC EDUCATION OFFICE
>   BUILDING 100
>   MAIL STATION U-614
>   P.O. BOX 90515
>   LOS ANGELES, CALIFORNIA   90009

Candidates must have at least a master's degree in a field of physical science, mathematics or engineering and rank in the top decile of the class. Awards may be work-study or full-time study in one of a number of major universities. Work assignments are primarily in southern California. Stipends are for one year but are renewable and range from $600 to $3,100 per academic year. In work-study situations the total financial benefits, including moving expenses, will range from $8,500 to $13,000 annually.

Typical Deadline: February 1

B-25   HUGHES MASTER'S FELLOWSHIPS (ENGINEERING, MATHEMATICS OR PHYSICS)

HUGHES AIRCRAFT COMPANY
SCIENTIFIC EDUCATION OFFICE
BUILDING 100
MAIL STATION U-614
P.O. BOX 90515
LOS ANGELES, CALIFORNIA   90009

Candidates must have a bachelor's degree in one of the above fields and a grade point average of at least B upon graduation. Financial aid can be a fellowship for full-time study or a work-study fellowship tenable primarily in southern California. Stipends range from $500 to $2,300 plus full salary for work performed. Applications are reviewed at any time, but usually four or five months prior to graduation.

B-26   DISSERTATION FELLOWSHIPS, RICHARD D. IRWIN FOUNDATION

THE RICHARD D. IRWIN FOUNDATION
1818 RIDGE ROAD
HOMEWOOD, ILLINOIS   60430

A small number of dissertation year grants for potential teachers in business, economics and the social sciences are made on nomination by the Graduate School Dean.

Typical Deadline: February 1

B-27   RICHARD M. WEAVER FELLOWSHIP AWARDS PROGRAM

INTERCOLLEGIATE STUDIES INSTITUTE, INCORPORATED
14 SOUTH BRYN MAWR AVENUE
BRYN MAWR, PENNSYLVANIA   19010

"Future teachers who are motivated by the need to integrate the idea of liberal education with their teaching, to restore to university studies their distinguishing and value-giving mark," may apply to the Institute for fellowships for graduate study. The Richard M. Weaver Fellowship provides a stipend of $2,000 and payment of tuition at the school of the recipient's choice. About 20 fellowships are awarded every year.

B-28   JACKSON LABORATORY COOPERATIVE GRADUATE STUDY PROGRAM (SCIENCES)

        THE ASSISTANT DIRECTOR (TRAINING)
        THE JACKSON LABORATORY
        BAR HARBOR, MAINE   04609

    The Jackson Laboratory is devoted to basic research into the role
of heredity in mammalian diseases and behavior. In addition to a small
summer program for a few graduate and medical students, the Laboratory
offers a cooperative graduate study program enabling graduate students to
do their thesis research throughout the year at the Laboratory. Limited
scholarship support is available for students in the summer program. No
funds are available for full-time students.

                                        Typical Deadline: July 9

B-29   KOSCIUSZKO FOUNDATION - POLISH STUDIES AND EXCHANGE SCHOLARSHIPS

        THE KOSCIUSZKO FOUNDATION
        15 EAST 65th STREET
        NEW YORK, NEW YORK   10021

    The Foundation administers several endowed scholarships for
academic and professional studies. The focus is on Polish studies, with
emphasis on assistance to Americans of Polish extraction. Many professional
fields as well as the arts and sciences are described in their printed
summary of financial aids. Scholarships are usually for one academic year
beyond the bachelor's degree. Any American student, regardless of national
extraction, is eligible for aid to study courses in Polish language or
literature. M.A. candidates with a knowledge of the Polish language may
compete for scholarships for study in Poland. These cover transportation,
tuition, room and board.

                                        Typical Deadline: January 1

B-30   ART HISTORY FELLOWSHIPS, ADVANCED GRADUATE RESEARCH

        THE METROPOLITAN MUSEUM OF ART
        NEW YORK, NEW YORK   10028

    The Museum has a limited number of fellowships. These are offered
to students who have a least an M.A. and often a doctorate in art history,
and who wish to carry out a specific research project on the collections of
the Museum. The term of the fellowship is ordinarily one year and the
stipend is usually $6,000 for a year. Renewal for a second year is possible.
Inquiries should be directed to the office of the Vice-Director for Education.

B-31 POST-BACCALAUREATE GRANTS AND AWARDS IN MUSIC

       MUSIC EDUCATORS NATIONAL CONFERENCE
       1201 SIXTEENTH STREET, N.W.
       WASHINGTON, D. C.   20036

    This publication lists foundation and trust awards, contests, auditions, etc., as well as financial aids available through graduate schools of music. This forty-page booklet is available as #321-10140 at a cost of two dollars from the above address.

B-32 DIRECTORY OF ASSISTANTSHIPS AND FELLOWSHIPS FOR GRADUATE STUDY
      IN ENGLISH AND THE TEACHING OF ENGLISH

       NATIONAL COUNCIL OF TEACHERS OF ENGLISH
       1111 KENYON ROAD
       URBANA, ILLINOIS   61801

    Edited by Linda K. Harvey, this publication is available for $2.50 and is designed to help students and teachers find financial assistance for graduate study in English and the teaching of English. Listed are opportunities for study in about 350 graduate departments. Published annually in November as a special issue of College Composition and Communication.

B-33 SEMINAR FOR HISTORICAL ADMINISTRATORS

       NATIONAL TRUST FOR HISTORIC PRESERVATION
       740-748 JACKSON PLACE, N.W.
       WASHINGTON, D. C.   20006

    Although no financial aid is available for formal study, the National Trust for Historic Preservation in cooperation with the American Association of Museums, the American Association for State and Local History and Colonial Williamsburg conducts annual six-week summer seminars for selected graduate students with a minimum of one year of graduate training in American history, American studies, American art and architectural history or allied fields and beginning professionals in the field. The seminar is tuition free and offers 18 fellowships with stipends of $500 each.

                        Typical Deadline: March 15

B-34   NATIONAL WILDLIFE FEDERATION CONSERVATION FELLOWSHIPS

         EXECUTIVE DIRECTOR
         NATIONAL WILDLIFE FEDERATION
         1412 SIXTEENTH STREET, N.W.
         WASHINGTON, D. C.   20036

    The applicant must be accepted as a candidate for a doctoral
degree at an accredited university as of the September following the time
of the award. The study areas must have a conservation emphasis. The
awards are for nine months and valued at $4,000 depending upon need.

                                        Typical Deadline: December 31

B-35   NEW YORK BOTANICAL GARDEN FELLOWSHIPS

         ADMINISTRATOR OF GRADUATE STUDIES
         THE NEW YORK BOTANICAL GARDEN
         BRONX, NEW YORK   10458

    The New York Botanical Garden offers several Graduate Fellowships
in systematic botany and related fields. Each fellow devotes half time to
formal graduate study leading to a Ph.D. degree at Lehman College of the
City University of New York (CUNY) and half time to herbarium or laboratory
assistance and to special assignments in systematic or floristic researches
at the Botanical Garden, including possible tropical expeditions. The
stipend is $4,450 a year plus tuition payment. Fellowships may be renewed
annually, contingent on satisfactory scholastic progress.

                                        Typical Deadline: March 1

B-36   NEW YORK CITY URBAN FELLOWSHIP PROGRAM

         DIRECTOR URBAN FELLOWSHIP PROGRAM
         OFFICE OF THE MAYOR
         250 BROADWAY
         NEW YORK, NEW YORK   10007

    Twenty "working fellowships" are awarded to seniors and graduate
students to work with city government officials in diverse assignments.
Each Urban Fellow must be granted appropriate academic credit by his college
or university and receive a supplemental grant of $500 from that college or
university. The City stipend is $4,000 plus travel expenses. Assignments
involve such areas as city planning, human rights, housing, health and
social services, budgeting, police science, youth services, etc.

                                        Typical Deadline: January 31

B-37   THE POPULATION COUNCIL FELLOWSHIPS

    THE FELLOWSHIP SECRETARY
    THE POPULATION COUNCIL
    245 PARK AVENUE
    NEW YORK, NEW YORK   10017

    Fellowships for a year of full-time study are available to citizens
of all countries, with preference to those candidates from less developed
areas. In addition, predoctoral and postdoctoral fellowships are offered
for special training in demography as well as relevant fields such as
sociology, economics and biostatistics. The plan of study and choice of
university is made by the applicant, with Council assistance as needed.
Fellowships are also offered by the Technical Assistance Division to
candidates professionally qualified as medical doctors, health educators,
social workers, nurses and social scientists who are interested in further
studies related to family planning, including research and evaluation of
family planning programs. Preference is given to those connected with
action programs in family planning with the assurance that they will be
reassigned to the programs upon return to their home countries. Similar
aid is available through Biomedical Division for those with advanced
degrees and research interests related to reproductive physiology.

                    Typical Deadline: Demographic - December 1
                                       Technical Assistance - December 15
                                       Biomedical - December 1

B-38   NATURAL RESOURCES DOCTORAL DISSERTATION FELLOWSHIPS

    RESOURCES FOR THE FUTURE, INCORPORATED
    FELLOWSHIP PROGRAM
    1755 MASSACHUSETTS AVENUE, N.W.
    WASHINGTON, D. C.   20036

    The purpose of these fellowships is to assist qualified graduate
students in completing doctoral dissertation work and to stimulate their
interest in the application of social science disciplines to problems of
natural resources. The fellowships, valued at more than $4,000, are
designed to enable selected students who have completed all doctoral
requirements except the dissertation to devote full time for one academic
year to dissertation research. The academic department nominates the
candidate, and the proposed research must relate to natural resources and
pertain to the social sciences.

                    Typical Deadline: February 1

B-39   SOCIAL SCIENCES DISSERTATION FELLOWSHIPS

GRADUATE STUDENT FELLOWSHIP PROGRAM
RUSSELL SAGE FOUNDATION
230 PARK AVENUE
NEW YORK, NEW YORK   10017

A very limited number of resident Fellowships are awarded annually to students in their final year of doctoral studies in the social sciences. Fellows are expected to spend half-time completing their doctoral dissertations and half-time participating in Foundation activities and may elect either a nine- or eleven-month period of residence. The stipend is $450 per month, plus cost of living allowance of $400 per month ($500 per month if Fellow has more than two dependents). In addition, $1,000 is made available to each Fellow for research and professional travel expenses. Fees required by Fellow's university to maintain degree candidate status are paid by the Foundation. Letter of nomination by a faculty member, plus two additional letters of reference, and letter of application from candidate accompanied by a curriculum vita should be sent to Dr. David A. Goslin, Chairman, Graduate Student Fellowship Program.

Typical Deadline: January 30

B-40   RUSSELL SAGE RESIDENCIES IN LAW AND SOCIAL SCIENCE

DIRECTOR
LAW AND SOCIAL SCIENCE RESIDENCY PROGRAM
RUSSELL SAGE FOUNDATION
230 PARK AVENUE
NEW YORK, NEW YORK   10017

This program is designed to help social scientists and lawyers equip themselves to do research on legal institutions and legal processes through use of the concepts and methods of social sciences. Applicants must have completed the doctorate or all requirements for the doctorate except the dissertation in sociology, psychology, anthropology, political science or history or have received a law degree. Appointments are made for an academic year with the possibility of a second year renewal and stipends range from $5,000 to $9,000 plus tuition.

Typical Deadline: December 1

B-41   SOCIETY OF EXPLORATION GEOPHYSICISTS SCHOLARSHIPS

        SOCIETY OF EXPLORATION GEOPHYSICISTS FOUNDATION
        P.O. BOX 3098
        TULSA, OKLAHOMA   74101

        In addition to awards for undergraduates, the Society awards a
limited number of scholarships to graduate students whose studies are
directed toward a career in exploration geophysics, in operations, teaching
or research. Awards include loans and grants-in-aid, but funds are limited
by lack of endowment and the need to rely upon annual contributions from
companies and individuals. Awards are $500 to $1,000 per year; most are
for $750. Applications must be received by March 1 of the year the award is
made.

B-42   ATOMIC ENERGY COMMISSION THESIS AND DISSERTATION LABORATORY
          GRADUATE PARTICIPATION

        UNIVERSITY PROGRAMS OFFICE
        OAK RIDGE ASSOCIATED UNIVERSITY
        P.O. BOX 17
        OAK RIDGE, TENNESSEE   37830

        These awards provide opportunities for master's and doctoral degree
candidates to conduct graduate thesis or dissertation research in established
programs at Atomic Energy Commission and other approved laboratories. The
basic stipend is $3,000 per calendar year plus a relocation allowance. Write
to the above address for further information.

B-43   U. S. ARMY MEDICAL SERVICE CORPS, GRADUATE STUDENT PROGRAM IN
          PSYCHOLOGY

        PSYCHOLOGY CONSULTANT
        OFFICE OF THE SURGEON GENERAL
        DEPARTMENT OF THE ARMY
        WASHINGTON, D. C.   20314

        This program is available to graduate students who have completed
at least one year of graduate work in psychology. Ph.D. candidates in
clinical or counseling psychology may receive an immediate commission with
full pay and allowances. Upon obtaining the Ph.D., the candidate must
serve as a staff psychologist in the Army. The U. S. Navy offers a somewhat
similar program for clinicians. Further information on this program may be
secured from The Bureau of Medicine and Surgery, Department of the Navy,
Washington, D.C.   20390.

B-44   HIGHER EDUCATION PERSONNEL TRAINING PROGRAMS

> DIVISION OF UNIVERSITY PROGRAMS
> BUREAU OF HIGHER EDUCATION
> U. S. OFFICE OF EDUCATION
> WASHINGTON, D.C.   20202

These Fellowships are allocated to institutions under Part E of the Educational Professions Development Act of 1967, which amends Title V of the Higher Education Act of 1965, and are for one or two years depending on the requirements of the approved programs. Fellowships are allocated to graduate programs for the training of two- and four-year college teachers below the doctoral level, and non-teaching higher education personnel (administrators and education specialists) at all levels. Stipends are $3,000 per year plus tuition and dependency allowances. A list of programs is available at the address above.

B-45   NDEA GRADUATE FOREIGN LANGUAGE FELLOWSHIPS (VI)

> U. S. DEPARTMENT OF HEALTH, EDUCATION AND WELFARE
> DIVISION OF FOREIGN STUDIES
> INSTITUTE OF INTERNATIONAL STUDIES
> OFFICE OF EDUCATION
> WASHINGTON, D. C.   20202

Fellowships are available for graduate work leading to either a master's degree or the Ph.D.   The awards are primarily to students who plan to teach foreign languages and related studies at the college level. Universities select the candidates, and applications should be obtained directly from graduate schools offering approved programs. For a list of participating institutions, write to the address above. (Due to funding difficulty, there is future uncertainty about this program.)

B-46   LAW ENFORCEMENT RESEARCH FELLOWSHIPS

> OFFICE OF EDUCATIONAL AND MANPOWER ASSISTANCE
> LAW ENFORCEMENT ASSISTANCE ADMINISTRATION
> 633 INDIANA AVENUE, N.W.
> WASHINGTON, D. C.   20530

Applicants must be enrolled in a doctoral program with all course work and preliminary examinations completed before the award will be made. The fellowship award is made to support the student's dissertation research. The research must relate to a criminal justice concern and preferably one that pertains to manpower. Further information may be secured from the address above.

                                        Typical Deadline: April 1

B-47   U. S. OFFICE OF EDUCATION SUPPORT FOR THE ARTS AND HUMANITIES

> SUPERINTENDENT OF DOCUMENTS
> U. S. GOVERNMENT PRINTING OFFICE
> WASHINGTON, D. C.   20402

The U.S. Office of Education administers a variety of legislative programs which may provide support for educational undertakings in the arts and humanities. The first part of this booklet is a summary of pertinent legislation arranged by title and section. The second presents a brief description of the assistance or program offered, who may apply, etc. It should be emphasized that none of the legislation cited provides support exclusively for arts and humanities programs or projects. (Price - 35 cents, Catalog Number HE5.2:AR7/5/72)

B-48   NATIONAL GALLERY OF ART FELLOWSHIPS

> NATIONAL GALLERY OF ART
> WASHINGTON, D. C.   20565

The National Gallery of Art awards fellowships in the history of art to students pursuing advanced degrees in this subject. The fellowships are usually granted to predoctoral candidates who have passed their general examinations and who have substantially advanced their thesis topics, normally through a year or more of research beyond the completion of their course requirements. Application deadline is January 31 of each year, for 12-month grants beginning on October 1.

B-49   NATIONAL SCIENCE FOUNDATION GRADUATE FELLOWSHIPS

> FELLOWSHIP OFFICE
> NATIONAL RESEARCH COUNCIL
> 2101 CONSTITUTION AVENUE, N.W.
> WASHINGTON, D. C.   20418

These three-year fellowships are available to beginning graduate students and to those who will have completed not more than one year of graduate study (irrespective of field) at the time they propose to begin fellowship tenure. Awards are made for study or work leading to master's or doctoral degrees in the mathematical, physical, medical, biological, engineering and social sciences and in the history and philosophy of science. Awards are not made in clinical, education or business fields, or in history or social work, or for work leading to medical, dental, law or joint Ph.D. professional degrees. Stipends are $3,600 for a 12-month tenure, irrespective of level of study; no dependency allowance is provided. Tenures are 9 or 12 months. A limited travel allowance is available. For further details, see program announcement which can be obtained from above address in late September.

Typical Deadline: November 26

B-50   GRANTS FOR IMPROVING DOCTORAL DISSERTATIONS IN THE FIELD SCIENCES

          DIVISION OF BIOLOGICAL AND MEDICAL SCIENCES
          NATIONAL SCIENCE FOUNDATION
          WASHINGTON, D. C.   20550

     These grants are intended to improve the quality of doctoral
dissertations in the field sciences, such as systematics, ecology and
biological oceanography. Funds may be used for travel to specialized
libraries, museums or field research locations, or for costs of specialized
equipment used in connection with field work, computer time and for field
research expense. Applications may be submitted at any time on behalf of
the graduate student by the dissertation advisor, department chairman or
departmental graduate chairman.

B-51   GRANTS FOR IMPROVING DOCTORAL DISSERTATION RESEARCH IN THE
          ENVIRONMENTAL SCIENCES

          DIVISION OF ENVIRONMENTAL SCIENCES
          NATIONAL SCIENCE FOUNDATION
          WASHINGTON, D. C.   20550

     These grants are intended to improve the scientific quality of
doctoral dissertations in the earth, atmospheric and oceanographic sciences.
Funds may be used for travel to specialized libraries, museums or field
research locations or for sample survey costs, equipment, microfilm, etc.
Applications on behalf of a graduate student who is at the point of
initiating dissertation research should be submitted by the advisor,
department chairman or departmental graduate chairman. There are no
deadlines, but four months should be allowed for normal processing.

B-52   DOCTORAL DISSERTATION RESEARCH IN THE SOCIAL SCIENCES

          NATIONAL SCIENCE FOUNDATION
          DIVISION OF SOCIAL SCIENCES
          WASHINGTON, D. C.   20550

     Proposals may be submitted by universities in the United States on
behalf of doctoral candidates. The grants are awarded to improve the
scientific quality of social science doctoral dissertations and to make
possible the use of larger quantities of better quality data. Funds may
be used for travel, field research, sample survey costs, microfilms, etc.,
but may not be used as a stipend. Further information may be secured at
the address above.

B-53   SMITHSONIAN OPPORTUNITIES FOR RESEARCH AND STUDY IN HISTORY, ART, SCIENCE

OFFICE OF ACADEMIC STUDIES
SMITHSONIAN INSTITUTION
WASHINGTON, D. C.   20560

This publication outlines research opportunities and collections available for study at the Smithsonian Institution. Accompanying these descriptions are brief biographical sketches of professional staff members who can supervise students in the following areas: History of Science and Technology, American and Cultural History, History of Art, Anthropology, Evolutionary and Systematic Biology, Environmental Sciences, Tropical Biology and Physical Sciences. Within these fields, six- to twelve-month appointments with stipend, in residence at the Smithsonian, are awarded to postdoctoral scholars who generally are within five years of their degree, and to predoctoral candidates who have completed all the course work toward their degree. Limited support is available for graduate students, but at present no support is available for undergraduates. Short-term visitors to the Institution (2-4 weeks) are also supported to a limited extent.

B-54   VETERANS ADMINISTRATION PSYCHOLOGY TRAINING PROGRAM

VETERANS ADMINISTRATION
DEPARTMENT OF MEDICINE AND SURGERY
PSYCHOLOGY DIVISION 116C
WASHINGTON, D. C.   20420

Students who are enrolled in accredited Ph.D. programs in clinical or counseling psychology and are recommended by a participating institution are eligible for Standard Stipends from $3,660 to $6,790 per year depending on their academic and clinical backgrounds.   In addition, Block Placement Stipends are provided at the third and fourth levels which require a year's training experience with the agency. These are funded at $8,512 at the third level and $9,082 at the fourth level.

B-55   WILDLIFE MANAGEMENT RESEARCH GRANTS

WILDLIFE MANAGEMENT INSTITUTE
WIRE BUILDING
WASHINGTON, D. C.   20005

The Institute issues a limited number of grants-in-aid each year to graduate students for work conducted as part of their academic training. Grants are seldom issued for more than $1,200 to $1,500 and most applications should be for more modest sums, with a focus on wildlife management studies.

Typical Deadline: November 1

B-56   AMELIA EARHART FELLOWSHIP AWARDS (SCIENCE - AEROSPACE ONLY)

          ZONTA INTERNATIONAL
          59 EAST VAN BUREN STREET
          CHICAGO, ILLINOIS   60605

     Grants of $3,000 are competitively awarded to women recommended
for their character and scholastic record and holding a bachelor's degree
in science acceptable as preparatory for advanced aerospace studies.

                                    Typical Deadline: January 1

B-57   GRANTS AND AID TO INDIVIDUALS IN THE ARTS

          WASHINGTON INTERNATIONAL ARTS LETTER
          1321 4th STREET, S.W.
          WASHINGTON, D. C.   20024

     The second edition of this publication contains listings of most
professional awards and information about colleges, universities and
professional schools of the arts which offer assistance to students in
amounts of $1,000 or more. It is indexed by discipline. ($10.95)

SPECIFIC CROSS REFERENCES

In addition to the references preceding, <u>every</u> candidate for financial aid is urged to read Section G in toto. This section describes financial aid publications, as well as important loan funds and grants which are not restricted to specific areas of graduate or professional study.

C   Social Services

The <u>Occupational Outlook Handbook</u> (G-29) points out that the development of a more complex urban society has greatly increased the need for organized social services. "The problems which concern social workers include poverty; broken homes; physical, mental and emotional handicaps; antisocial behavior; racial tensions; and unsatisfactory community conditions such as inadequate housing and medical care, and lack of educational, recreational, and cultural opportunities." In the past, traineeships were made available to graduate programs relating to social services through Federal government funding. Since 1971, however, there has been a general policy to curtail Federal funds for specialized manpower training programs. It is anticipated that by 1974 general student aid programs administered by the Office of Education will fill this gap. These programs will provide scholarship assistance for needy students at the undergraduate level and guaranteed loans for both undergraduate and graduate students.

C-1   SOCIAL GROUP WORK - KLUTZNICK SCHOLARSHIPS

>   B'NAI B'RITH YOUTH ORGANIZATION
>   1640 RHODE ISLAND AVENUE, N.W.
>   WASHINGTON, D. C.   20036

College seniors planning to enter a school of social work and intending to major in group work may apply for grants in the amount of $2,000 or $2,500 per year with the understanding that they are expected to work for at least two years with BBYO upon completion of their schooling.

C-2   <u>FAMILY SERVICE GRANTS TO STUDENTS IN GRADUATE SCHOOLS OF SOCIAL WORK</u>

>   FAMILY SERVICE ASSOCIATION OF AMERICA
>   44 EAST 23rd STREET
>   NEW YORK, NEW YORK   10010

This pamphlet provides a list of grants available from family service agencies. Candidates must be accepted for admission to a graduate school of social work. The individual listings are by state and by agency and include the benefits and restrictions.

C-3   SCHOLARSHIPS, FELLOWSHIPS, WORK-STUDY PLANS FOR GRADUATE SOCIAL WORK EDUCATION

> PERSONNEL SERVICES
> NATIONAL JEWISH WELFARE BOARD
> 15 EAST 26th STREET
> NEW YORK, NEW YORK   10010

This pamphlet was compiled for individuals interested in careers in Jewish Community Centers and YM-YWHA's and is available upon request at the address above.

Typical Deadline: April 1

C-4   CAREER AND TRAINEESHIP INFORMATION FOR GRADUATE STUDY IN REHABILITATION COUNSELING

> NATIONAL REHABILITATION COUNSELING ASSOCIATION
> 1522 K STREET, N.W.
> WASHINGTON, D. C.   20005

A 1972 revision of the pamphlet Career and Traineeship Information for Graduate Study in Rehabilitation Counseling is available at the address above. Also available is a list of graduate schools in the United States offering Rehabilitation Counselor Education.

C-5   DEPARTMENT OF JUSTICE ACADEMIC ASSISTANCE GRANTS (LEEP)

> LAW ENFORCEMENT ASSISTANCE ADMINISTRATION
> U. S. DEPARTMENT OF JUSTICE
> WASHINGTON, D. C.   20530

Under the Department of Justice's Law Enforcement Education Program (LEEP), funds are provided to encourage qualified men and women to enter or continue in the field of law enforcement. Full-time students who are enrolled in a degree program directly related to law enforcement may qualify for up to $2,200 per academic year to cover tuition and related expenses. For those already employed full-time in a law enforcement agency (police, courts or corrections) grants of up to $400 per semester are available for further study. Loans are forgiven at the rate of 25 per cent a year for those who become a certified full-time employee in a criminal justice agency; grants need not be repaid if the recipient remains in full-time criminal justice employment for two years. Applications for loans and grants are made directly to the college or university that the student would like to attend. A list of participating schools may be obtained by writing to the address above.

C-6   TRAINEESHIPS IN SOCIAL WORK

CHIEF
STAFF DEVELOPMENT AND EDUCATION DIVISION
SOCIAL SERVICE WORK (122)
DEPARTMENT OF MEDICINE AND SURGERY
VETERANS ADMINISTRATION
WASHINGTON, D. C.   20420

Master's and doctoral students enrolled in an accredited school of social work may apply to their dean for a stipend and placement in a Veterans Administration hospital or clinic. Stipends of $2,900 to $6,000 depending on years of study are offered.

SPECIFIC CROSS REFERENCES

In addition to the references preceding, every candidate for financial d is urged to read Section G in toto. This section describes financial d publications, as well as important loan funds and grants which are not stricted to specific areas of graduate or professional study.

D   Professional Study in Health-Related Fields

The probability that some form of national health insurance for all citizens will become a reality through congressional legislation in the early 1970's will spotlight the need for a significant increase in the educational preparation of professionals and paraprofessionals in all fields related to health.

In addition to the myriad of professionally trained persons needed fo direct health care, including such relatively new positions as physician's assistant, there will be a corresponding need for research and teaching personnel in professional schools, as well as for basic scientific researc

D-1   ADMISSION REQUIREMENTS OF AMERICAN DENTAL SCHOOLS

THE AMERICAN ASSOCIATION OF DENTAL SCHOOLS
1625 MASSACHUSETTS AVENUE, N.W.
WASHINGTON, D. C.   20036

This annual publication is available each September at a cost of four dollars and in addition to listing information about all dental schoc in the United States and Canada includes detailed information on financi aids available from each of these schools.

D-2   DENTAL APTITUDE TEST

DIVISION OF EDUCATIONAL MEASUREMENTS
COUNCIL ON DENTAL EDUCATION
AMERICAN DENTAL ASSOCIATION
211 EAST CHICAGO AVENUE
CHICAGO, ILLINOIS   60611

The American Dental Association sponsors three tests each year fo applicants to dental schools. The testing program requires one full day's attendance at the testing center, and each center offers the test on Saturday. The dates are usually in April, October and January. All denta schools give the test on all dates, as do some larger colleges and universities. An information booklet and application may be secured from campus dental school advisors or the address above.

D-3   AMERICAN MEDICAL ASSOCIATION EDUCATION AND RESEARCH FOUNDATION
        STUDENT LOAN PROGRAM

        AMERICAN MEDICAL ASSOCIATION
        535 NORTH DEARBORN STREET
        CHICAGO, ILLINOIS   60610

        Enrolled medical students, or interns or residents in full-time
training, may borrow up to $1,500 per year. During training interest
accrues. A maximum of ten years for repayment begins after training is
ended. Information and application forms are available from the medical
school or hospital to which the applicant has been accepted.

D-4   HORIZONS UNLIMITED

        AMERICAN MEDICAL ASSOCIATION
        535 NORTH DEARBORN STREET
        CHICAGO, ILLINOIS   60610

        This is an excellent career guide for all health-related
professions, and has some value in the field of financial aids through a
chapter on financing a medical education. It has references in each
occupational area to professional associations where information on
financial aids for the specialization is usually available. The eighth
edition was published in November of 1970 and single copies are available
without charge.

D-5   OCCUPATIONAL THERAPY

        AMERICAN OCCUPATIONAL THERAPY FOUNDATION
        6000 EXECUTIVE BOULEVARD
        ROCKVILLE, MARYLAND   20852

        The Foundation awards a limited number of scholarships each year
for study in occupational therapy; other sources such as loans are also
available. Students should write to the above address to obtain more
information concerning the types of financial aid available from the
foundation.

D-6   FINANCIAL AIDS FOR OPTOMETRY STUDENTS

        AMERICAN OPTOMETRIC ASSOCIATION
        7000 CHIPPEWA STREET
        ST. LOUIS, MISSOURI   63119

        This pamphlet lists scholarships and loan funds which are available
for the study of optometry.

D-7   EDUCATION ANNUAL (THE JOURNAL OF THE AMERICAN OSTEOPATHIC
         ASSOCIATION MARCH 1973)

         OFFICE OF EDUCATION
         AMERICAN OSTEOPATHIC ASSOCIATION
         212 EAST OHIO STREET
         CHICAGO, ILLINOIS   60611

         Persons interested in the osteopathic profession and its training
should obtain the EDUCATION ANNUAL of the JOURNAL OF THE AMERICAN
OSTEOPATHIC ASSOCIATION, March issue from the address above. (Single
copies free.) This publication contains information about applicants for
each year's class in considerable detail. There is also a four-page
description of various types of financial aid, as well as a description of
the osteopathic curriculum and descriptions of the colleges and affiliated
hospitals. Also included in this publication is information on students'
loan funds of the American Osteopathic Association and the National
Osteopathic Foundation, an osteopathic licensing summary, federation
licensing examination information, information on the National Board of
Examiners for Osteopathic Physicians and Surgeons, Inc., intern registrati
program, hospital requirements for residency training in osteopathic
specialties, osteopathic hospitals accredited for intern and residency
training, requirements for certification: Advisory Board for Osteopathic
Specialists and Boards of Certification, prerequisites and requirements fo
earned fellowship in the American Academy of Osteopathy, postdoctoral gran
available through the National Osteopathic Foundation, osteopathic researc
grants administered through the AOA Bureau of Research, continuing medical
education and other general information on the profession.

D-8   NATIONAL OSTEOPATHIC COLLEGE SCHOLARSHIPS

         AMERICAN OSTEOPATHIC ASSOCIATION
         OFFICE OF EDUCATION
         212 EAST OHIO STREET
         CHICAGO, ILLINOIS   60611

         Sponsored by the AOA Auxiliary, these scholarships (about 27) are
valued at $750 for the freshman year and may be renewed for $750 the
sophomore year of study in one of the seven approved colleges of osteopath
medicine. Academic record, need, motivation, citizenship in the United
States or Canada and acceptance in one of the seven approved colleges of
osteopathic medicine are factors in these awards.

                                        Typical Deadline: May 1

D-9   CAREERS IN PHYSICAL THERAPY

> AMERICAN PHYSICAL THERAPY ASSOCIATION
> 1156 15th STREET, N.W.
> WASHINGTON, D. C.   20005

This publication of the Association describes employment opportunities, licensing and registration requirements, the certification programs for graduates in arts and sciences and the master's programs. In addition, more than 50 accredited programs in colleges, medical schools and universities are listed. There is also a two-page listing of sources of financial aid. Single copies are available without charge at the address above.

D-10   AMERICAN PODIATRY ASSOCIATION FELLOWSHIPS

> AMERICAN PODIATRY ASSOCIATION
> COMMITTEE ON SCHOLARSHIPS AND FELLOWSHIPS
> 20 CHEVY CHASE CIRCLE, N.W.
> WASHINGTON, D. C.   20015

This brochure gives a description of the APA fellowship program. Six awards of $4,000 each are available each year for graduate study in a field related to podiatry, such as basic and clinical sciences, public health, education and educational administration. Recipients must work at a college of podiatric medicine a minimum of four hours a week or a total of 120 hours during summer months.

D-11   STUDENT FINANCIAL AID IN SPEECH PATHOLOGY AND AUDIOLOGY

> AMERICAN SPEECH AND HEARING ASSOCIATION
> 9030 OLD GEORGETOWN ROAD
> WASHINGTON, D. C.   20014

This pamphlet describes major Federal aid programs and some sources of private funds for study in speech pathology and audiology.

D-12   <u>MEDICAL SCHOOL ADMISSION REQUIREMENTS, U. S. A. AND CANADA</u>

> ASSOCIATION OF AMERICAN MEDICAL COLLEGES
> ATTN: MEMBERSHIP AND SUBSCRIPTIONS
> ONE DUPONT CIRCLE, N.W.
> WASHINGTON, D. C.   20036

Chapter 4, "Financial Information for Undergraduate and Medical Students," describes in general terms such categories as student expenses, microscope requirement, nonrefundable aid, Health Professions Scholarship Program, loans, etc. This annual publication costs four dollars.

D-13   COLLEGES OF PODIATRY ADMISSION TEST

> COLLEGES OF PODIATRY ADMISSION TEST
> EDUCATIONAL TESTING SERVICE
> 960 GROVE STREET
> EVANSTON, ILLINOIS   60201

This is a three-hour test used by the five American colleges of podiatric medicine in selecting students for full-time study and is given in October, February and June. Four scores are reported to all the colleges: (1) Verbal Aptitude, (2) Quantitative Aptitude, (3) Natural Science and (4) Spatial Relationships. An information bulletin and application are available from the nearest college or university or ETS.

D-14   INSTITUTE OF FOOD TECHNOLOGY GRADUATE FELLOWSHIPS

> INSTITUTE OF FOOD TECHNOLOGY
> SUITE 2120
> 221 NORTH LA SALLE STREET
> CHICAGO, ILLINOIS   60601

Information about schools offering programs in the science and technology of food and some of the scholarships and fellowships may be secured from the address above. However, the actual applications must be forwarded only by the head of the department in which the student is alrea enrolled.

D-15 WHERE TO GET HEALTH CAREER INFORMATION

          NATIONAL HEALTH COUNCIL, INCORPORATED
          1740 BROADWAY
          NEW YORK, NEW YORK   10019

     This pamphlet, available without charge from the Council, lists
5 professional associations and government agencies from which information
ay be obtained by persons considering professional study in a health-
elated specialization. Most of the source agencies could be expected to
upply current information about careers, financial aids, training programs,
tc.

-16 SCHOLARSHIPS, FELLOWSHIPS, EDUCATIONAL GRANTS AND LOANS FOR
     REGISTERED NURSES

          NATIONAL LEAGUE FOR NURSING
          10 COLUMBUS CIRCLE
          NEW YORK, NEW YORK   10019

     This pamphlet gives sources of funds for registered nurses planning
ork toward baccalaureate, master's or doctoral degrees.

-17 NEW YORK STATE REGENTS SCHOLARSHIPS FOR MEDICINE, DENTISTRY
     AND OSTEOPATHY

          REGENTS EXAMINATION AND SCHOLARSHIP CENTER
          STATE EDUCATION DEPARTMENT
          99 WASHINGTON AVENUE
          ALBANY, NEW YORK   12210

     There are 80 awards annually for the study of medicine, and 20
nnually for the study of dentistry, available for study within New York
ate (or professional study of osteopathy in the United States). Half of
ch type are awarded to New York City residents and the other half to
ndidates residing elsewhere in the state. The scholarships are for four
ars in the amount of $350 to $1,000 per year, depending on need. Citizen-
ip and residence requirements prevail. Eligible candidates must be in
ll-time attendance at an approved preprofessional college during the year
 competition; have not previously taken the examination; not be enrolled
 schools of medicine, dentistry or osteopathy, and must have completed the
quired preprofessional courses prior to the effective date of the scholar-
ip. Applications must usually be filed by October 8 of the final academic
ar.

D-18   MEDICAL COLLEGE ADMISSION TEST

        MEDICAL COLLEGE ADMISSION TEST
        THE PSYCHOLOGICAL CORPORATION
        304 EAST 45th STREET
        NEW YORK, NEW YORK   10017

    As a part of the application process, most medical schools request
the score on the Medical College Admission Test. This examination is given
twice yearly, and is usually taken in October or May of the year preceding
graduation.

    It is designed to measure general academic ability, general
information and scientific knowledge. Scores are released only to medical
schools. There are test centers throughout the country. Further informatio
and applications are available from campus premedical advisors or the
address above.

D-19   ARMED FORCES HEALTH PROFESSIONS SCHOLARSHIP PROGRAM

        U.S. ARMY
        DEPARTMENT OF THE ARMY
        DASG-PTP
        WASHINGTON, D. C.   20314

        U.S. NAVY
        BUREAU OF MEDICINE AND SURGERY
        NAVY DEPARTMENT (CODE 3174)
        WASHINGTON, D. C.   20372

        U.S. AIR FORCE
        ATC/RSOS
        RANDOLPH AIR FORCE BASE, TEXAS   78148

    The Uniformed Services Health Professions Revitalization Act of
1972 (Public Law 92-426) established 5000 scholarships for students in the
health services. This number has been divided between the Army, Navy and
Air Force and will be given to students in medicine, osteopathy, dentistry,
veterinary medicine, optometry, podiatry and clinical psychology at the
Ph.D. level.

    Basically, the program known as the Armed Forces Health Professions
Scholarship Program is as follows: an eligible student applies to one of
the three branches of the Armed Forces of his choice. If selected he is
commissioned a second lieutenant or ensign in the inactive reserve. While
in the program the student receives a stipend of $400.00 per month, except
during an annual 45-day active duty tour for which he will receive
approximately $1,080.00. The active duty tour will be performed at a
military hospital or medical center and will be arranged in order not to
interrupt the student's academic work. If required by the school, arrange-

ments may be made to permit the active duty to be performed on campus. In
addition, the service will pay all tuition, mandatory fees and related
academic expenses of the student.

The student incurs an obligation of one year of active commissioned
service for each year or fraction of a year of program participation. All
participants incur a minimum tour of two years.

For further information concerning the Armed Forces Health
Professions Scholarship Program, you may write one of the above addresses.

D-20   AIR POLLUTION FELLOWSHIPS

MANPOWER DEVELOPMENT STAFF
CONTROLLED PROGRAMS DEVELOPMENT DIVISION
OFFICE OF AIR QUALITY PLANNING AND STANDARDS
RESEARCH TRIANGLE PARK, NORTH CAROLINA   27711

At present 55 graduate students are being supported by Air Pollution
Control Office Fellowships for study in air pollution control. The average
assistance is $6,500. For further information write to the address above.

D-21   NATIONAL INSTITUTES OF MENTAL HEALTH SUPPORT PROGRAMS

U. S. DEPARTMENT OF HEALTH, EDUCATION AND WELFARE
U. S. PUBLIC HEALTH SERVICE
NATIONAL INSTITUTES OF MENTAL HEALTH
5600 FISHERS LANE
ROCKVILLE, MARYLAND   20852

New guidelines are being developed for the NIMH grant support
programs in research, training and services. The revised publication will
be available in 1974. Information about specific programs can be obtained
from the Mental Health Staff at the DHEW Regional Offices in Boston,
Massachusetts; New York City, New York; Philadelphia, Pennsylvania; Atlanta,
Georgia; Chicago, Illinois; Dallas, Texas; Kansas City, Missouri; Denver,
Colorado; San Francisco, California; and Seattle, Washington; and from the
NIMH central office.

D-22   NURSING SCHOLARSHIPS, FELLOWSHIPS, STUDENT LOANS AND TRAINEESHIPS

U. S. DEPARTMENT OF HEALTH, EDUCATION AND WELFARE
DIVISION OF NURSING
BUREAU OF HEALTH MANPOWER EDUCATION
NATIONAL INSTITUTES OF HEALTH
BETHESDA, MARYLAND   20014

Nursing students enrolled in public and nonprofit private schools
of nursing are eligible for educational aid in the form of loans and
scholarships. Registered nurses are eligible for traineeships to prepare
as teachers, supervisors, administrators and specialists in certain
clinical areas. Nurses with baccalaureate preparation may apply for
Fellowships to prepare for research in nursing and health-related
scientific fields.

D-23   HEALTH PROFESSIONS SCHOLARSHIPS

U. S. DEPARTMENT OF HEALTH, EDUCATION AND WELFARE
BUREAU OF HEALTH MANPOWER EDUCATION
NATIONAL INSTITUTES OF HEALTH
BETHESDA, MARYLAND   20014

Under Section 780-781, Public Health Service Act, as amended,
students with exceptional financial need enrolled in participating health
professions schools pursuing a full-time course of study required to become
a physician, dentist, osteopath, optometrist, pharmacist, podiatrist or
veterinarian may apply for a scholarship of up to $3,500 per academic year.
Applicants should contact the financial aid office of the school where
they have been accepted for enrollment or are enrolled.

D-24   HEALTH PROFESSIONS STUDENT LOANS

U. S. DEPARTMENT OF HEALTH, EDUCATION AND WELFARE
BUREAU OF HEALTH MANPOWER EDUCATION
NATIONAL INSTITUTES OF HEALTH
BETHESDA, MARYLAND   20014

Under Section 740-746, Public Health Service Act, as amended,
financially needy students enrolled in participating health professions
schools pursuing a full-time course of study required to become a physician
dentist, osteopath, optometrist, pharmacist, podiatrist or veterinarian
may apply for long-term, low-interest health professions loans of up
to $3,500 per academic year. Portions of the loans may be waived for
practice in a shortage area following graduation. Students should contact
the financial aid office at the school where they have been accepted for
enrollment or are enrolled.

-25   BUREAU OF SPORTS FISHERIES AND WILDLIFE

            SEE BELOW

        The Fish and Wildlife Service, Bureau of Sport Fisheries and Wild-
life, does not offer a program of financial aid to students. However, the
ureau administers and partially supports Cooperative Fishery and Wildlife
nits at 20 colleges and universities where many graduate students receive
ome type of support administered by the schools. A publication "Cooperative
ishery Unit Report for the 1969-70 School Year," Resource Publication 90 of
he United States Department of the Interior, describes these programs and
he research of graduate students in the programs. It is available from the
uperintendent of Documents for 60 cents.

-26   TRAINEESHIPS IN MEDICAL LIBRARIANSHIP AND BIOMEDICAL COMMUNICATION

            RESEARCH, TRAINING, AND PUBLICATIONS DIVISION
            EXTRAMURAL PROGRAMS
            NATIONAL LIBRARY OF MEDICINE
            8600 ROCKVILLE PIKE
            BETHESDA, MARYLAND   20014

        Under the Medical Library Assistance Act, there is a training
rogram for biomedical librarians and related health communications
pecialists. Support is provided in the form of grants to training
rograms at qualified institutions. The training program directors select
he trainees. For applicants with a baccalaureate degree there are
urrently programs leading to the M.S. or M.A. degree in the management
f health sciences information systems, biomedical communications (including
nformation storage and retrieval systems) and other aspects of health
cience librarianship. There are also programs at the doctoral and post-
octoral level. An outline of programs currently supported is available
t the address above.

-27   STIPEND AWARDS FOR GRADUATE AUDIOLOGY AND SPEECH PATHOLOGY
            TRAINING

            CHIEF
            AUDIOLOGY AND SPEECH PATHOLOGY
            VETERANS ADMINISTRATION CENTRAL OFFICE
            810 VERMONT AVENUE, N.W.
            WASHINGTON, D. C.   20420

        Applicants must have at least a bachelor's degree and be enrolled
 an accredited program of audiology or speech pathology. Tax-free
tipend awards range from $3,320 to $6,000 per year depending on the level
 graduate study. Write to the address above for further information.

D-28   OPTOMETRY COLLEGE ADMISSION TEST

         OPTOMETRY COLLEGE ADMISSION TEST
         THE PSYCHOLOGICAL CORPORATION
         304 EAST 45th STREET
         NEW YORK, NEW YORK   10017

The Association of Schools and Colleges of Optometry sponsors three tests each year for applicants to optometry schools. Testing dates are usually in November, January and March. An information booklet and application may be secured from the address above.

SPECIFIC CROSS REFERENCES

In addition to the references preceding, every candidate for financial aid is urged to read Section G in toto. This section describes financial aid publications, as well as important loan funds and grants which are not restricted to specific areas of graduate or professional study.

E Other Fields of Professional Study
Business and Public Administration
Education
Journalism
Law
Library Science
Theology
Urban Planning

Business and Public Administration

More than 25,000 students receive master's degrees yearly in specializations relating to management of various types of enterprises, and an additional 700 doctoral degrees are awarded. Schools granting these advanced degrees have traditionally carried the title of "Graduate School of Business," but some are known as "Graduate School of Public Administration," or a combination title which may include both terms or be known as "Graduate School of Management," or "Business and Economics," "Industrial Administration," "Administrative Science," "Business and Technology " and many similar titles.

Within these schools there are such specializations as accounting, finance, statistics, economics, management, marketing, labor economics, international business, data processing, taxation, quantitative analysis, long-term planning, urban problems, personnel administration, health care administration, procurement and contracting, transportation, production management, organizational behavior, risk management and insurance, etc. Some schools have a common core of courses in the first year, with individual programs to meet given student needs and interests in the second year. There are also joint programs in law.

Even though the names of the schools have management and administration as common denominators, and the M.B.A. or M.S. or Ph.D. degrees are those commonly awarded, there are many significant differences between schools in their educational philosophy and objectives, and considerable research should be undertaken by the person considering this type of graduate study. The three major resources are Peterson's Guides available in most colleges and universities; Graduate Study in Management: A Guide for Prospective Students (see E-5) and, of course, the individual school catalogs.

E-1   FELLOWSHIP PROGRAM IN ACCOUNTING

          AMERICAN ACCOUNTING ASSOCIATION
          653 SOUTH ORANGE AVENUE
          SARASOTA, FLORIDA   33577

     Students who will have completed a year of graduate study in accounting or business and expect to receive a doctor's degree and teach accounting may compete for one of the fellowships, which are valued at $1,000 to $3,000 for a year of study. Acceptance in a doctoral program at a school accredited by the AACSB is necessary.

                                        Typical Deadline: March 1

E-2   GRANTS-IN-AID FOR DOCTORAL DISSERTATIONS IN ACCOUNTING

          COMMITTEE ON RELATIONS WITH UNIVERSITIES
          AMERICAN INSTITUTE OF CPA's
          666 FIFTH AVENUE
          NEW YORK, NEW YORK   10019

     An applicant must be working for a doctorate at a school that is a member of the American Association of Collegiate Schools of Business and intend to become a teacher of accounting. The grants provide $450 per month for single persons or $500 per month for married persons for a maximum of twelve months. Grants are to be used for preparation of the dissertation. Candidates may obtain further information and details about application procedures at the address above.

                                        Typical Deadline: March 1

E-3   DISSERTATION FELLOWSHIPS - ACCOUNTING

>   DIRECTOR OF PERSONNEL
            ARTHUR ANDERSEN & COMPANY
            69 WEST WASHINGTON STREET
            CHICAGO, ILLINOIS   60602

        Prospective accounting teachers who are candidates for the doctoral
degree and at the dissertation stage may apply for one-year fellowships to
complete the dissertation. The fellowships provide $500 per month for a
single person or $550 per month for a married person plus any required
tuition. There is a moral obligation to either teach accounting at the
college level or repay the fellowship.

                                      Typical Deadline: March 1

E-4   ADMISSION TEST FOR GRADUATE STUDY IN BUSINESS

            ADMISSION TEST FOR GRADUATE STUDY IN BUSINESS
            EDUCATIONAL TESTING SERVICE
            BOX 966
            PRINCETON, NEW JERSEY   08540

        Offered four times each year, the ATGSB is a three-and-a-half hour
aptitude test designed to measure certain mental capabilities important in
the study of business at the graduate level. It is not a "subject matter"
test. A bulletin of information listing test dates, test centers, sample
questions and an application are available from the nearest college,
university or by writing to ETS.

E-5   GRADUATE STUDY IN MANAGEMENT: A GUIDE FOR PROSPECTIVE STUDENTS

            ADMISSION TEST FOR GRADUATE STUDY IN BUSINESS
            EDUCATIONAL TESTING SERVICE
            BOX 966
            PRINCETON, NEW JERSEY   08540

        Published annually and prepared by the Graduate Business Admissions
Council, this book is designed to provide information for prospective
graduate students and their counselors which will help them in making
decisions about beginning the study of business at the graduate level and
about the selection of a school. Included are descriptions of more than
280 graduate business school programs that require the Admission Test for
Graduate Study in Business. This publication also contains a full-length
sample of the ATGSB as well as information on special programs such as
public and educational administration, hospital/health care, urban planning,
and combined business-law degrees. Graduate Study in Management is
available for $3.50 per copy and can be ordered by writing directly to the
ATGSB Program at ETS.

E-6   GRADUATE FELLOWSHIPS - INSURANCE EDUCATION

        S. S. HUEBNER FOUNDATION FOR INSURANCE EDUCATION
        COLONIAL PENN CENTER
        3641 LOCUST WALK
        PHILADELPHIA, PENNSYLVANIA   19174

A successful applicant for a Foundation grant will be required to certify that (1) it is his intention to follow an insurance teaching career, (2) he will major in risk and insurance for a graduate degree and (3) during the period for which he holds a fellowship he will not engage in any outside work for pay or profit without the consent of the Executive Director. To be eligible for a predoctoral fellowship, an applicant must be a citizen of the United States or Canada, be under 35 years of age and have obtained a baccalaureate degree from an accredited college or university. A person in his senior year of undergraduate work may apply for a grant to be effective in the following year contingent upon satisfaction of the degree requirements. Predoctoral fellowships provide for: (1) a monthly cash stipend of $450 for a married candidate with a child or children and $400 for all other recipients and (2) the tuition and other fees of the Graduate School of Arts and Sciences. Summer fellowships, available upon evidence of satisfactory progress, provide income at the same rate as that payable during the regular academic year, as well as payment of tuition and fees. Thus, a fellowship holder may receive a nontaxable income up to $5,400 during a twelve-month period and have tuition and fees of $3,420 paid on his behalf, the potential value of the fellowship for one year being $7,820.

                                    Typical Deadline: February 1

E-7   DOCTORAL RESEARCH GRANTS, NATIONAL ASSOCIATION OF PURCHASING
         MANAGEMENT

        DOCTORAL RESEARCH GRANT SELECTION COMMITTEE
        NATIONAL ASSOCIATION OF PURCHASING MANAGEMENT
        11 PARK PLACE
        NEW YORK, NEW YORK   10007

A limited number of fellowships are available annually to doctoral candidates pursuing graduate study in purchasing materials management, management's procurement obligation and related fields. The amount of the basic stipend is $3,600 for one academic year. In addition, up to $1,400 may be granted to cover research expenses connected with the dissertation.

                                    Typical Deadline: February 1

E-8   SOUTHERN REGIONAL TRAINING PROGRAM IN PUBLIC ADMINISTRATION

            EDUCATIONAL DIRECTOR
            SOUTHERN REGIONAL TRAINING PROGRAM
            DRAWER I
            UNIVERSITY, ALABAMA   35486

        The Southern Regional Training Program, sponsored by the
Universities of Alabama, Kentucky and Tennessee is designed to train persons
for a career in public administration in the South. Fellowships involve a
stipend of $3,300 (single) or $3,700 (married) plus tuition and fees. The
program involves a summer internship in a southern governmental agency and
a nine-month academic program at two of the three universities.

                                    Typical Deadline: March 1

Education

Persons interested in training to work in the profession of education in the 1970's will find it extremely important to study for advanced graduate and professional degrees in their field of interest. Candidates preparing for customary positions in elementary and secondary schools, public and private, have little opportunity for financial aid other than in the form of loans or internships through various M.A.T. programs administered by departments or schools of education.

Although most statistics point to an existing oversupply of teachers, shortages still prevail in a few teaching areas. Special education with its emphasis on training educational personnel to meet the needs of handicapped children is one of these. In addition there is a short supply of graduates of education programs in mathematics, industrial arts, reading, distributive education, drug education and counseling. The current emphasis on "career education" will create a demand for specialists in this area and the trend towards more stimulating and pragmatic teaching techniques and environments will provide a need for information and media specialists.

E-9   FINANCIAL AID FOR GUIDANCE AND PERSONNEL GRADUATE STUDY

> THE AMERICAN PERSONNEL AND GUIDANCE ASSOCIATION
> 1607 NEW HAMPSHIRE AVENUE, N.W.
> WASHINGTON, D. C.   20009

Listed in this publication are graduate schools and departments offering programs in school and college counseling, school psychology, educational psychology, evaluation and measurement, counseling the emotionally disturbed child, pastoral counseling, student personnel administration, social and rehabilitation services, etc., together with the type, number and amounts of financial aids available. 58 pp. $5.50.

E-10   GRADUATE FELLOWSHIPS FOR WOMEN

          THE DANFORTH FOUNDATION
          222 SOUTH CENTRAL AVENUE
          ST. LOUIS, MISSOURI   63105

     Eligible for the 35 appointments yearly are women who are pro-
spective teachers at the secondary or college level, with at least a
bachelor's degree, but whose career has been interrupted for at least
three years. Applications may propose full- or part-time study at the
master's or doctoral level. Apply directly to the Foundation.

                                        Typical Deadline: Early January

E-11   SPECIAL EDUCATION

          (THE GRADUATE SCHOOLS OF NEARLY ALL MAJOR UNIVERSITIES IN THE
          UNITED STATES)

     Because the area of special education is growing rapidly and there
appears to be no central source of funding, students in Arts and Sciences
should be aware that they are eligible for direct admission to a wide variety
of graduate programs designed to train teachers to serve students with
special needs. Among these are graduate programs to train teachers of the
mentally retarded, the emotionally disturbed, the multiple handicapped, the
physically handicapped and the perceptually handicapped. Some Federal
traineeships are offered, and there are some paid internships and other
financial aids. Contact with several graduate schools is recommended. See
also other resources listed in this section.

E-12   TRAINEE-FELLOWSHIP PROGRAM IN SPECIAL EDUCATION

          DEPARTMENT OF SCHOLARSHIP SERVICES
          STATE OF ILLINOIS
          OFFICE OF THE SUPERINTENDENT OF PUBLIC INSTRUCTION
          SPRINGFIELD, ILLINOIS   62706

     Under Article 14 of "The School Code of Illinois" and Public Law
85-926 as amended, the state of Illinois has developed a unique system of
financial aid for students studying in special education fields in colleges
in the State of Illinois, both public and private. Professional worker
classifications are in the fields of: Educable Mentally Handicapped.
Trainable Mentally Handicapped, Socially Maladjusted, Learning Disabilities,
Emotionally Disturbed, Multiple Handicapped, Partially Seeing, Blind, Deaf,
Preschool Deaf, Hard of Hearing, Physically Handicapped, Physical Therapist,
Occupational Therapist, Speech Correction, School Psychologist, School
Psychologist Intern, School Social Work, Supervision, Administration and
Prevocational Counselor.

E-13   MOTT FELLOWSHIPS IN COMMUNITY EDUCATION

        MOTT LEADERSHIP CENTER
        1017 AVON STREET
        FLINT, MICHIGAN   48503

        The concept of community education is based on the premise that
education should be relevant to people's needs and that local resources can
be united to solve community problems. The Clinical Preparation Program
for Educational Leadership is a cooperative venture of seven of the state
universities in Michigan, the Mott Foundation and the Flint Community
Schools and combines graduate study with intern leadership experience.
College students (and educators at all levels) may apply. Those applying
for master's degree Fellowships must furnish evidence of a firm intent to
become Community School Directors. A doctoral fellow receives $8,000, and
a master's fellow receives $5,000 for a one year period.

                                            Typical Deadline: December 15

E-14   MILLER ANALOGIES TEST

        THE PSYCHOLOGICAL CORPORATION
        304 EAST 45th STREET
        NEW YORK, NEW YORK   10017

        The Miller Analogies Test (MAT) is often used in support of
admission to graduate schools. This 50-minute test consists of 100 analogies
arranged in order of difficulty. Appointments to take this test may be
individually arranged at one of the many testing centers listed in a
pamphlet available at the address above.

E-15   TEACHER CORPS

        DIRECTOR
        TEACHER CORPS
        U. S. DEPARTMENT OF HEALTH, EDUCATION AND WELFARE
        BUREAU OF EDUCATIONAL PERSONNEL DEVELOPMENT
        OFFICE OF EDUCATION
        WASHINGTON, D. C.   20202

        The Teacher Corps program aims to improve the educational
opportunities for children of low-income families by attracting able college
graduates to the teaching profession. The program provides on-the-job
training for two years in a poverty area school and concurrent graduate
study in a nearby university. Applications are reviewed and selection
determined by funded local Teacher Corps programs. Selections are usually
made in the late spring or early summer. Teacher Corps projects begin at
varying starting dates throughout the summer.

E-16   EDUCATION OF HANDICAPPED CHILDREN SCHOLARSHIP PROGRAM

          U. S. DEPARTMENT OF HEALTH, EDUCATION AND WELFARE
          OFFICE OF EDUCATION
          BUREAU OF EDUCATION FOR THE HANDICAPPED
          DIVISION OF TRAINING PROGRAMS
          WASHINGTON, D. C.   20202

          This publication describes the undergraduate scholarships and
traineeships and the graduate fellowships available for full-time study in
areas of education for the handicapped. To assist applicants in determining
where to apply for aid, a directory is provided which lists state educational
agencies and institutions to which direct application may be made.

E-17   HIGHER EDUCATION PERSONNEL TRAINING PROGRAMS 1973-1974:
          FELLOWSHIP PROGRAMS

          EPDA PART E FELLOWSHIP PROGRAM
          GRADUATE ACADEMIC PROGRAMS BRANCH
          BUREAU OF HIGHER EDUCATION
          U. S. OFFICE OF EDUCATION
          WASHINGTON, D. C.   20202

          This booklet describes programs administered by various universities
to train teachers, administrators and educational specialists for careers
in higher education, usually at the two-year college level, awarding a
master's degree in most instances. In addition to academic fields, these
programs cover training in such areas as remedial education, nursing,
college student personnel work, law enforcement, business management,
engineering technology, hotel and restaurant administration, environmental
science, library science, etc. Write to the address above for publication
OE 58028-72.

E-18   HIGHER EDUCATION PERSONNEL TRAINING PROGRAMS 1973-1974:
          INSTITUTES AND SHORT-TERM TRAINING PROGRAMS

          DIVISION OF COLLEGE SUPPORT
          BUREAU OF HIGHER EDUCATION
          U. S. OFFICE OF EDUCATION
          WASHINGTON, D. C.   20202

          The training programs listed in this booklet are funded under
Part E of the Education Professions Development Act of 1967. The only
general requirement for admission to an institute or short-term training
program is the applicant's capability for undertaking graduate-level training, but directors establish any special admission requirements. The 122
programs listed are primarily concerned with the training of educational
personnel in many facets of working with minority groups in such fields as

drug education, faculty development, counseling, Chicano studies, security, group awareness, financial aids, etc. For further information, write to the address above.

Journalism

Although "journalism" is defined as "the work of gathering news for, writing for, editing, or directing the publication of a newspaper or other periodical,"[1] modern graduate schools of journalism are better described as having programs in mass communications. Various departments and schools now carry such titles as "Communication," "Public Communication," "Center for Advancement of Human Communication," "Graduate School of Corporate and Political Communication," "Communications and Theater," "Radio-Television Film," "Mass Communication," "Radio, Television and Motion Pictures," etc. Equipment may include photographic laboratories, radio and television studios, complete film facilities, composing rooms, communications research libraries, computer centers, speech sciences laboratory, facilities for simultaneous translation of languages, video tape recorders, etc.

The programs of study, involving two to four semesters, include such possible specialized areas as political and government reporting, broadcasting, film, journalism, communication research, science communication, public relations, broadcast journalism, advertising, magazine work, public opinion, editorial interpretation of contemporary affairs, urban problems, the legal system, science and technology, the educational system, the arts, mental health information, religious journalism, media research, etc.

Most schools offer loans, part-time employment, work-study, internships, graduate assistantships, fellowships, grants-in-aid, tuition waivers or some combination of these.

(1) Webster's New World Dictionary of the American Language, College Edition, New York: The World Publishing Company, (1968).

JOURNALISM SCHOLARSHIP GUIDE

THE NEWSPAPER FUND
P.O. BOX 300
PRINCETON, NEW JERSEY   08540

Schools, newspapers, professional societies and journalism-related
foundations offer more than two million dollars in financial aid for college
students who want to study journalism. These four sources of scholarships,
fellowships and assistantships are fully described in the above-mentioned
publication. In addition there is a section on aid for minority group
students and information on tuition costs in all colleges and universities
which have full departments of journalism. Single copies are available
without charge from the address above.

<u>Law</u>

The number of applicants to law school have dramatically increased and any person interested in becoming a lawyer is urged to read the publication listed below. (E-20)

E-20   <u>PRE-LAW HANDBOOK</u>: <u>OFFICIAL LAW SCHOOL GUIDE</u>

ASSOCIATION OF AMERICAN LAW SCHOOLS
SUITE 370
ONE DUPONT CIRCLE, N.W.
WASHINGTON, D. C.   20036

The Association, in conjunction with the Law School Admission Council, prepares and publishes this book annually. It contains general information on the legal profession and legal education, including financial aid, as well as descriptions of individual law schools. The book, which is highly recommended for any person considering law as a career, is available for sale from LSAT/LSDAS, Educational Testing Service, Box 944, Princeton, New Jersey 08540.

E-21   <u>FINANCIAL AIDS FOR LAW STUDENTS</u>

INFORMATION SERVICE
AMERICAN BAR ASSOCIATION
1155 EAST 60th STREET
CHICAGO, ILLINOIS   60637

In March of 1970, the Information Service of the American Bar Association published a four-page pamphlet concerning financial aids. With their permission, much of this material is reproduced below:

The Information Service and the Law Student Division of the American Bar Association has compiled this information to answer the many inquiries received from college students who are contemplating law school.

The office of the dean of the law school or the office of financial assistance of the college or university of which the law school is a part is the student's best source of information on financial aid. This compilation can only suggest to the student the avenues of financial aid that are open to him since the situation will vary from year to year and between law schools. It is hoped by the Association that no prospective law student will allow lack of financial means to keep him from attending law school until every avenue of financial aid has been investigated.

The prospective law student faced with heavy financial commit-

ents or lack of funds may not need to forego law school or divide his time
y taking a part-time job while attending school. The investigation of all
f the avenues of financial assistance should be undertaken by any student
onsidering law school.

Legal educators agree that studying law is a full-time commitment.
he distraction of a part-time job, which most three-year law schools
estrict to a low paying 20 hours per week, is costly even after graduation
hen initial earnings tend to be proportionate to academic standing. For
any, those with a family to support for instance, a full-time job and four
ears of evening school may be the only answer.

The average annual total expenditures for private law school
tudents living away from home runs from $2,000 to $3,000 or more. Scholar-
hip grants and loans may not be expected to cover this entire amount for
ny but the most outstanding students, the most generous scholarships
sually being in the amount of full tuition. Pre-law students should plan
heir future expenditures carefully so that they can predict accurately the
mount of financial aid that they will need. Once a realistic goal has been
stablished, the search may start for the most suitable among the many kinds
f financial aid available.

The best source of complete and up-to-date information on
inancial assistance is the office of the dean of the law school or the
ffice of financial assistance of the college or university of which the
aw school is a part.

Prospective law students may also find it worthwhile to consult
he various directories of financial aids, which are available in most
ollege libraries, although these are bound to be incomplete as the number
f aids available changes yearly.

Scholarships

Scholarships are the most sought after grants-in-aid and the
ompetition for available scholarship assistance is always keen. Usually
tudents who maintain a high academic standing may look forward to
eceiving these outright grants-in-aid. At present, only about one-tenth
f the nation's 70,000 law students may expect to receive this type of aid
n the amount of $500 or more annually. In addition to full tuition grants,
ome scholarships provide for maintenance in university dormitories; some
rovide an additional amount for travel expenses for students from distant
arts of the country; and, in some cases, cash awards are made. Some
cholarships are available to students of certain ethnic or religious
ackgrounds, to women students, or handicapped students, as stipulated by
rivate donors. We are listing some of these special-group scholarships
ere. Most scholarships are administered by the law schools and information
oncerning them may be obtained in school catalogues and from the admissions
ffices of schools.

Not to be overlooked by the prospective scholarship applicant,
ut frequently more difficult to locate are those aids given by various
rganizations or individuals directly to the student without any university
r law school administration whatsoever. Such donors are: church groups;

veterans' organizations; county and state bar associations; law wives'
groups, (alumni or students); various ethnic organizations; corporations
with special programs for their employees; and local branches of alumni
societies of particular schools. By inquiring of the organizations to
which he and his family belong, a student will obtain information about
such scholarships for which he might be eligible. For information about
bar-related programs, students who live in a large community might get in
touch with their local bar association; those living in small communities
might write to the state bar association in the capital city in their state

"Regional" or "Waiver of Tuition" Scholarships

Most aids are granted to upperclassmen only, because schools can
never be certain, in advance of admission, that the student will make the
academic grade, regardless of his scores on aptitude tests or his undergraduate record. There are some schools which have scholarships available
to entering students, usually those who have maintained high academic
standing throughout their undergraduate studies. Among these are the
"regional" or "waiver of tuition" scholarships. These are provided by a
growing number of law schools, especially those of a "national" character
which draw their student body from the country at large. They enable a
law school to attract qualified freshmen from all over the United States,
thus broadening the educational experience of the student body and
improving the calibre of the school's graduates. This type of scholarship
is usually financed by solicitation of law firms or alumni in the
geographic area from which the entering student comes. Thus the school
does not actually forego tuition; it is compensated for the tuition cost
by donations.

Since advance knowledge of the existence of these regional
scholarships might influence the choice of schools to which pre-law studen
might apply and since it is impossible to generalize about the location of
these scholarships, we are listing them here. Excluded are those scholarships which are available to residents of the state in which the law schoo
is located, since the majority of schools have one or more such scholarshi
available. The information listed is complete,...(but) scholarship
offerings change from year to year.

Loan Fund Programs

For the majority of law students who cannot qualify for scholarship aid on the basis of need, academic standing, or other special
stipulation, there are substantial loan funds available. In 1965, the
American Bar Association instituted such a loan fund, which is one aspect
of the bar's work toward an expanded program for the support of legal
education in the United States and part of its continuing effort to
attract promising students to the study of law. As with most financial ai
programs, applications should be made through the law school.

Additional...funds are available to veterans through the Veteran
Administration, and law students are eligible to receive assistance under
the National Direct Student Loan Program, administered through law schools
The federal government has a program to insure loans granted by banks and
other financial institutions, as do many of the individual states. Many
states also have loan funds available, especially for students attending

aw schools affiliated with state universities.

Before applying for any loan, students are urged to investigate ll sources of aid and compare their terms. They should not assume, ecause funds are provided through their school, that their terms are the est available. Many banks, loan institutions and insurance companies have lans specifically designed to meet the needs of students. Although these ompanies are profit making organizations, they may be able to extend ong-range financial assistance specifically suited to an individual tudent's needs through their wide resources, at terms lower than those vailable through a university. After investigating and comparing the ossible avenues to financial assistance, it would be wise for the student o consult the financial or loan advisor at his university before making ny commitments.

Other Aids

Although prizes and awards cannot be counted on to contribute to he support of a law student, they can be a source of income to the winner. wards are frequently made for outstanding work in a particular subject, nd there are a number of essay competitions open to law students, such s the ABA Law Student Division's annual competitions in Opinion Letter riting or International Law. In addition to the financial prize involved, he winning of an award or contest may favorably influence prospective mployers. The extra work entailed may pay surprising dividends.

Work scholarships are offered by a number of schools, usually to tudents who need but cannot otherwise qualify for aid. These scholar-hips, which provide for work in libraries, dining rooms or administrative ffices, should not be relied upon as a major source of income, since the ompensation is not great and the schools discourage their students from orking more than a minimal number of hours.

Low tuition is another form of aid, with the taxpayer paying the ifference between cost and tuition (in the case of state-operated chools), or with the deficit being paid by the contributions of private onors (in the case of private law schools). Tuition rates are published nnually in the "Review of Legal Education," which is available from the merican Bar Association to college students interested in entering law chool.

E-22   LAW SCHOOL ADMISSION TEST

          LAW SCHOOL ADMISSION TEST
          EDUCATIONAL TESTING SERVICE
          BOX 944
          PRINCETON, NEW JERSEY   08540

This test is required by about 190 law schools and is given in
October, December, February, April and July. Scholarship applicants are
urged to register for the October or December administrations. Scores are
often helpful for advisory purposes, therefore, many law school applicants
would probably benefit by taking the test late in their junior year or very
early in their senior year. The test requires a half day. A booklet of
information, which also describes the new Law School Data Assembly Service an
the Graduate and Professional School Financial Aid Service, is available
from the nearest college, university or from the address above.

E-23   LAW SCHOOL DATA ASSEMBLY SERVICE

          LAW SCHOOL DATA ASSEMBLY SERVICE
          EDUCATIONAL TESTING SERVICE
          BOX 944
          PRINCETON, NEW JERSEY   08540

Developed by the Law School Admission Council and administered by
Educational Testing Service, the Law School Data Assembly Service (LSDAS)
is designed to simplify admissions procedures for applicants to
participating law schools. (See also Law School Admission Test and the
Graduate and Professional School Financial Aid Service.)

E-24   GRADUATE AND PROFESSIONAL SCHOOL FINANCIAL AID SERVICE

          GRADUATE AND PROFESSIONAL SCHOOL FINANCIAL AID SERVICE
          EDUCATIONAL TESTING SERVICE
          BOX 2614
          PRINCETON, NEW JERSEY   08540

A service of the Graduate and Professional Financial Aid Council
administered by Educational Testing Service, the GAPSFAS is designed to
provide financial aid officers of participating graduate and professional
schools with an analysis of the financial resources of all applicants. The
form for 1974-75 is designed to serve as an application for financial
assistance at those schools participating in GAPSFAS. Current information
and application forms are available from the address above. (See also Law
School Data Assembly Service and Law School Admission Test.)

Library Science

A nationwide shortage of trained librarians is expected to continue, despite the anticipated rise in the number of library school graduates, according to Occupational Outlook Handbook.[1] The same publication points out that the increased financial assistance to school and public libraries is increasing the need for services, as are expanding student populations. Industry needs special librarians and science information specialists, and as new methods of storing and retrieving information by computer are developed, more well-trained librarians are needed.

The undergraduate preparation for application to a school of library science is customarily the bachelor's degree. Reading knowledge of a foreign language is required by many schools. Scores on the Graduate Record Examination (B-17) are often required. The program of study leads to a master's degree and usually may be completed within an academic or calendar year. Various specializations include those for careers in public libraries, school libraries, newspaper libraries, international libraries, documentation and communication centers, information storage and retrieval, reference service, cataloging, information science, etc.

Each school of library science has differences in curriculum and financial aids, which include those in sources cited below.

1) U. S. Department of Labor, Bureau of Labor Statistics, Bulletin No. 1650, for sale by the U.S. Government Printing Office, Washington, D. C. 20402 at $6.25.

E-25   FINANCIAL ASSISTANCE FOR LIBRARY EDUCATION, ACADEMIC YEAR
         1974-75

         AMERICAN LIBRARY ASSOCIATION
         LIBRARY EDUCATION DIVISION
         50 EAST HURON STREET
         CHICAGO, ILLINOIS   60611

     This annual publication is a listing of awards from state library
agencies, state professional groups and awards of institutions offering
programs in library education. Assistance from foundation and governmental
agencies is included, and there is a current listing of graduate library
schools accredited by the American Library Association.

E-26   SPECIAL LIBRARIES ASSOCIATION SCHOLARSHIP PROGRAM

         SPECIAL LIBRARIES ASSOCIATION
         SCHOLARSHIP COMMITTEE
         235 PARK AVENUE SOUTH
         NEW YORK, NEW YORK   10003

     A limited number of scholarships valued at $2000 each are awarded
by the Special Libraries Association for graduate study leading to a
master's degree at a recognized school of library or information science
in the U.S. or Canada. Preference is given to United States citizens
interested in pursuing a career in special librarianship.

                                        Typical Deadline: January 15

Theology

Arts and sciences students who are contemplating a career in theology should be aware that clerical training in either the Protestant ministry, the Jewish rabbinate or the Roman Catholic priesthood requires at least three years of post-baccalaureate education. A student who is interested in this calling should first consult his own minister, rabbi or priest to obtain general information about the religious life. Financial aid for graduate study in this area is provided privately from the churches or synagogues and from the school that the student plans to attend.

E-27   THEOLOGICAL EDUCATION - TRIAL YEAR IN SEMINARY

        THE FUND FOR THEOLOGICAL EDUCATION, INCORPORATED
        RESEARCH PARK, BLDG. J
        1101 STATE ROAD
        PRINCETON, NEW JERSEY   08540

These awards are for one year and intended to be for a "trial year" during which time the Fellow seeks to determine whether the Protestant ministry is personally a viable vocation. The seventy Fellowships cover room, board, tuition, fees, etc. Candidates must be nominated by a minister, faculty member or former Fellow prior to November 20. Candidacy is open to men and women under thirty who are citizens of the United States or Canada and are seniors or recipients of a bachelor's degree. This program is designed to pay for the first year only.

Typical Deadline: November 20

Urban Planning

More than 50 colleges and universities award the master's degree in urban planning. Undergraduate degrees in most fields are acceptable preparation. Two years of graduate work are typically required, includin workshop, laboratory and studio courses, as well as economics, trans- portation, social systems, land planning, ecology, political science, public finance, minority relations, gerontology, sociology, recreation, cartography, etc. A paid summer experience is customary at many schools. There are also several doctoral level programs.

E-28   EDUCATION AND CAREER INFORMATION FOR PLANNING AND RELATED FIELDS

This 18-page pamphlet is a joint publication available from eith American Society of Planning Officials, 1313 East 60th Street, Chicago, Illinois 60637 or American Institute of Planners, 1776 Massachusetts Avenue, N.W., Washington, D. C. 20036. It provides a complete listing c colleges and universities offering planning and related programs and has brief sections on financial aids, educational preparation, a bibliography and sample employment opportunities. Available without charge at the addresses above.

SPECIFIC CROSS REFERENCES

In addition to the references preceding, <u>every</u> candidate for financial aid is urged to read Section G in toto. This section describes financial aid publications, as well as important loan funds and grants which are not restricted to specific areas of graduate or professional study.

F Financial Aid Available Only to Members of Minority Groups

Applicants qualified for, and interested in, the awards outlined below should also carefully review financial aid opportunities listed in other categories of this publication which relate to relevant graduate or professional study.

F-1   DENTAL SCHOLARSHIPS FOR UNDERGRADUATE MINORITY STUDENTS

         AMERICAN FUND FOR DENTAL EDUCATION
         SUITE 1630
         211 E. CHICAGO AVENUE
         CHICAGO, ILLINOIS   60611

An American Fund for Dental Education scholarship provides up to $12,500 for five years of schooling. It is possible to receive as much as $2,500 for the final year of pre-dental education in college and for each year of dental school. Any minority student, as defined by the AFDE program, who is preparing to enter his or her senior, junior or sophomore year in college is eligible to apply for an AFDE dental scholarship. Students entering dental school or already in dental school are not eligible Ambition is the main qualification, including: academic background, financial need and character. The deadline for applying is July 1 for study beginning in September.

F-2   JOURNALISM - INFORMATION ABOUT FINANCIAL AIDS

         AMERICAN NEWSPAPER PUBLISHERS
         ASSOCIATION FOUNDATION
         P.O. BOX 17407, DULLES INTERNATIONAL AIRPORT
         WASHINGTON, D. C.   20041

This organization offers financial aid for black and other minority students studying journalism at schools of journalism accredited by the American Council on Education for Journalism.

                              Typical Deadline: April

F-3   POLITICAL SCIENCE FELLOWSHIPS FOR BLACKS

         APSA GRADUATE FELLOWSHIPS FOR BLACK STUDENTS
         AMERICAN POLITICAL SCIENCE ASSOCIATION
         1527 NEW HAMPSHIRE AVENUE, N. W.
         WASHINGTON, D. C.   20036

    The Association is underwriting a limited number of fellowships
for blacks about to enter graduate school for the study of political
science. They also seek to identify other promising candidates who may be
eligible for financial aid from any university and to encourage institutions
to provide them with financial assistance.

                                   Typical Deadline: February 1

F-4   SPECIAL ASSISTANCE PROGRAMS FOR MINORITY GROUP STUDENTS OF
         SPEECH PATHOLOGY AND AUDIOLOGY

         AMERICAN SPEECH AND HEARING ASSOCIATION
         9030 OLD GEORGETOWN ROAD
         WASHINGTON, D. C.   20014

    This two-page pamphlet lists colleges and universities offering
some type of special assistance including tuition rebate, special
counseling or special financial aids in the field of speech pathology and
audiology to members of various minority groups or to those who are
academically disadvantaged.

F-5   GRADUATE STUDY - BUSINESS MANAGEMENT

         CONSORTIUM FOR GRADUATE STUDY IN MANAGEMENT
         101 NORTH SKINKER BOULEVARD
         BOX 1132
         ST. LOUIS, MISSOURI   63130

    Six cooperating universities, Indiana University, University of
North Carolina (Chapel Hill), University of Rochester, University of
Southern California, Washington University (St. Louis) and the University
of Wisconsin award fellowships to blacks, Puerto Ricans, Chicanos, Cubans
and American Indians interested in management careers in business. Fellowships include full tuition and a $2,000 stipend for the first year, plus
full tuition and $1,000 for the second year. There is also a Summer
Business Internship in the employ of a sponsoring business firm. The M.B.A.
is awarded. Prior study in business or economics is not a prerequisite.

F-6   FORD FOUNDATION GRADUATE FELLOWSHIPS

         GRADUATE FELLOWSHIPS (SPECIFIC ETHNIC GROUP)
         THE FORD FOUNDATION
         320 EAST 43rd STREET
         NEW YORK, NEW YORK   10017

    Fellowships are for Black Americans, Puerto Ricans, Mexican
Americans and Native Americans. Consideration will be given to (a) students
who are United States citizens; (b) students who plan to pursue full-time
study toward the doctoral degree in Arts or Sciences or applicants who hold
a first post-baccalaureate professional degree (MBA, MPA, MSW, M.Ed., etc.)
and plan to continue on to the doctoral degree in preparation for a career
in higher education; (c) applicants who are currently engaged in or plan to
enter a career in higher education. Fellowship awards include: full
tuition and fees, $300 book and supplies allowance and monthly stipend of
$250. These awards are for one year only but are renewable upon
reapplication and evidence of satisfactory progress. All applicants must
submit the Graduate Record Examination scores for the Aptitude and Advanced
Test. Applications are available at the above address.

                                        Typical Deadline: January 5

F-7   GRADUATE MANAGEMENT EDUCATION

         COUNCIL FOR OPPORTUNITY IN GRADUATE MANAGEMENT EDUCATION (COGME)
         CENTER PLAZA
         675 MASSACHUSETTS AVENUE
         CAMBRIDGE, MASSACHUSETTS   02139

    The Council provides graduate fellowships to members of minority
groups for enrollment in MBA programs at the following ten graduate schools
of management: University of California, Berkeley; Carnegie-Mellon
University; University of Chicago; Columbia University; Dartmouth College
(Amos Tuck School); Harvard University; Massachusetts Institute of
Technology; University of Pennsylvania (Wharton School); Stanford
University.

F-8   PRE-LAW SUMMER INSTITUTES

COUNCIL ON LEGAL EDUCATION OPPORTUNITY (CLEO)
2000 P STREET, N.W.
SUITE 300
WASHINGTON, D. C.   20036

In cooperation with the American Bar Association, the National Bar Association, the Association of American Law Schools, La Raza National Lawyers Association and the Law School Admission Council, CLEO sponsors several summer institutes at law schools throughout the country designed for disadvantaged and minority students who have received or are in the process of receiving the bachelor's degree and who plan to attend a law school in September. The programs vary with the sponsoring institution. The Council published on June 1, 1971 a pamphlet, "Financial Aid Programs for Minority Group Students in Law Schools," which may be obtained without charge at the address above.

Typical Deadline: Early March

F-9   GRADUATE AND PROFESSIONAL SCHOOL OPPORTUNITIES FOR MINORITY STUDENTS

The 1973 edition of Graduate and Professional School Opportunities for Minority Students contains information about more than 1600 graduate and professional schools and departments. Included are deadlines for admission and financial aid, admission test requirements, whether application fees may be waived and the percentages of minority students enrolled and receiving financial aid. Copies of this publication have been sent to most college, university and public libraries, undergraduate advisors and to various minority group organizations. If a library or organization convenient to you does not have a copy, please ask them to order it free of charge from the Special Services Section, Educational Testing Service, Princeton, New Jersey 08540.

F-10   THE PROTESTANT FELLOWSHIP PROGRAM

        THE FUND FOR THEOLOGICAL EDUCATION, INC.
        RESEARCH PARK, BUILDING J
        1101 STATE ROAD
        PRINCETON, NEW JERSEY   08540

Each candidate must be nominated by a clergyman or a faculty member
prior to November 20 of each year. The Fund offers financial aid to black
students committed to the Christian ministry. Candidates should be male,
under 30, have a good academic record and be in the junior or senior year
of the bachelor's program or attending a Protestant theological school.
The Fund also awards about 70 fellowships annually for "A Trial Year in
Seminary," with no racial or denominational restrictions.

                                        Typical Deadline: November 20

F-11   FINANCIAL SUPPORT FOR BLACK DOCTORAL CANDIDATES IN RELIGION

        ROCKEFELLER DOCTORAL FELLOWSHIPS IN RELIGION
        RESEARCH PARK, BUILDING J
        1101 STATE ROAD
        PRINCETON, NEW JERSEY   08540

This program seeks to strengthen Protestant theological education
in the U.S. by financially aiding twelve black Protestants per year who seek
the doctoral degree in religion and who evidence high promise of scholarship and teaching ability. Each candidate must be nominated by faculty
prior to February 21 of each year. Further information is available from
the above address.

F-12   BASIC MEDICAL SCIENCES

        DIVISION OF MEDICAL SCIENCES
        FACULTY OF ARTS AND SCIENCES
        HARVARD MEDICAL SCHOOL
        25 SHATTUCK STREET
        BOSTON, MASSACHUSETTS   02115

In 1974-75, the Division of Medical Sciences of the Faculty of
Arts and Sciences at Harvard Medical School will offer financial support to
admitted students who are members of minority groups. At least 15 graduate
candidates are sought for Ph.D. programs in the biological sciences.

F-13   STUDENT PERSONNEL ADMINISTRATION AT HOWARD UNIVERSITY

COORDINATOR
STUDENT PERSONNEL PROGRAM
BOX 205
HOWARD UNIVERSITY
WASHINGTON, D. C.   20001

Fifteen assistantships valued at $3,400 each will be awarded for the masters program in student personnel administration. These assistant-ships require 20 hours of work weekly in an area of student personnel services and are for a maximum of two years tenure.

Typical Deadline: May 1

F-14   BLACK STUDENTS IN INTERNATIONAL AFFAIRS

DEAN OF ADMISSIONS
SCHOOL OF ADVANCED INTERNATIONAL STUDIES
THE JOHNS HOPKINS UNIVERSITY
1740 MASSACHUSETTS AVENUE, N.W.
WASHINGTON, D. C.   20036

Graduate fellowships for blacks for M.A. or Ph.D. programs in international politics, African studies, economic development, comparative politics, international law and modern languages are offered by Johns Hopkins; they are valued at full tuition or up to $4,000. Other fellowships, also ranging up to $4,000, are available on the basis of financial need and academic merit.

Typical Deadline: February 15

F-15   THE EARL WARREN LEGAL TRAINING PROGRAM

THE EARL WARREN LEGAL TRAINING PROGRAM
10 COLUMBUS CIRCLE - SUITE 2030
NEW YORK, NEW YORK   10019

The purpose of the program is to increase the number of black lawyers in the United States, therefore, this program is designed to provide scholarships for 300 entering law students each year, and continued support through completion of the full three-year course of study is possible. The last class under this program will graduate in 1979. In addition to the academic year scholarships, selected law students will receive assistance with summer jobs in Legal Defense Fund offices as well as a post-graduate year of internship.

Typical Deadline: March 15

F-16   NATIONAL MEDICAL FELLOWSHIPS

>   NATIONAL MEDICAL FELLOWSHIPS, INCORPORATED
>   3935 ELM STREET
>   DOWNERS GROVE, ILLINOIS   60515

Students from minority groups currently underrepresented in the
medical profession, specifically, American blacks, Mexican Americans, main-
land Puerto Ricans and American Indians, who have been accepted by an
accredited medical school for study leading to the M.D. degree, are eligible
to apply if there is financial need. (In 1972-73, 1,518 grants were made
averaging $1,140.) Renewals are probable for the second year at approximately
the same level as the original grants.

Typical Deadline: April 1

F-17   SPECIAL SCHOLARSHIP PROGRAM IN LAW FOR AMERICAN INDIANS

>   SCHOOL OF LAW
>   UNIVERSITY OF NEW MEXICO
>   1915 ROMA, N.E.
>   ALBUQUERQUE, NEW MEXICO   87131

The University of New Mexico School of Law runs a special summer
program (after the bachelor's degree) for about 35 American Indian students,
who may subsequently enroll at the University's School of Law or any other
accredited law school to which they have been accepted. The summer program
is fully subsidized, and grants for the subsequent year of law school are
available, including an additional benefit for dependents, with a maximum
of $4,400 per year. Students must provide their own tuition if it is not
waived by the law school they attend.

F-18   JOURNALISM SCHOLARSHIP GUIDE

>   THE NEWSPAPER FUND
>   P.O. BOX 300
>   PRINCETON, NEW JERSEY   08540

Part II of the Guide is specifically devoted to scholarships for
members of minority groups. However, the book of nearly 100 pages is an
outstanding resource of all types of financial aid for the study of
journalism and is available without charge at the address above.

F-19   BEYOND HIGH SCHOOL: EDUCATIONAL OPPORTUNITIES AND FINANCIAL AID

        SCHOLARSHIP INFORMATION CENTER
        UNIVERSITY OF NORTH CAROLINA
        YMCA-YWCA
        CHAPEL HILL, NORTH CAROLINA   27514

    Although this publication is directed mostly to high school seniors,
there are some resources mentioned for graduate or professional study at
specific institutions. The booklet is free to high school seniors and
guidance counselors. The cost for others is one dollar.

F-20   LAW SCHOOLS AND MINORITY GROUPS

        SCHOLARSHIP INFORMATION CENTER
        UNIVERSITY OF NORTH CAROLINA
        YMCA-YWCA
        CHAPEL HILL, NORTH CAROLINA   27514

    This publication is a guide to opportunities in legal education for
members of minority groups. It includes data for most law schools on
minority enrollments, admissions and scholarships. The cost is one dollar.

F-21   FELLOWSHIPS IN MANAGEMENT AT NORTHWESTERN UNIVERSITY

        DIRECTOR OF ADMISSIONS
        GRADUATE SCHOOL OF MANAGEMENT
        NORTHWESTERN UNIVERSITY
        EVANSTON, ILLINOIS   60201

    Sponsoring companies provide fellowships and summer work opportuni-
ties for minority group students enrolling in the two-year Master of
Business Administration curriculum.

                                Typical Deadline: March 1

F-22   DOCTOR OF OPTOMETRY

          STATE UNIVERSITY OF NEW YORK
          STATE COLLEGE OF OPTOMETRY
          122 EAST 25th STREET
          NEW YORK, NEW YORK   10010

     The State University of New York State College of Optometry
operates a special minority recruitment program for its professional
program leading to the Doctor of Optometry degree. A minimum of two years
of college with a very good academic record is required for entrance,
however, most students entering have completed the bachelor's degree.

F-23   THE SOUTHERN FELLOWSHIP FUND

          THE SOUTHERN FELLOWSHIP FUND
          795 PEACHTREE STREET, N.W.
          ATLANTA, GEORGIA   30308

     A substantial grant by the Danforth Foundation is enabling the
Southern Fellowship Fund to provide financial aid to strengthen the
faculty and administrative staffs at colleges and universities attended
predominately by black students. There are predoctoral and dissertation-
year fellowships available to students who intend to enter college teaching
in similar colleges. Some previous teaching experience may be a factor in
selection.

                              Typical Deadline: December 15

F-24   TEACHERS COLLEGE SCHOLARSHIPS IN EDUCATION

          STUDENT INFORMATION CENTER
          TEACHERS COLLEGE - BOX 197
          525 WEST 120th STREET
          NEW YORK, NEW YORK   10027

     Teachers College, Columbia University offers special tuition
scholarships for one year of full-time study. Competition is limited to
citizens of the United States. The focus of the program is to attract to
the College, Puerto Rican, black and other minority group students who have
been "educationally disadvantaged."

                              Typical Deadline: February 1

F-25   SCHOLARSHIPS FOR AMERICAN INDIANS

> BUREAU OF INDIAN AFFAIRS
> BRANCH OF HIGHER EDUCATION
> 123 4th STREET, S.W.
> P.O. BOX 1788
> ALBUQUERQUE, NEW MEXICO   87103

Describing Federal and state aids, tribal aid grants and loan funds for American Indians, this pamphlet also lists a number of scholarships specifically for American Indian students in colleges and universities. Another section is devoted to scholarships from churches, foundations and other organizations.

F-26   ASPO-FORD FOUNDATION MINORITY FELLOWSHIP PROGRAM IN PLANNING

> ASPO-FORD FOUNDATION FELLOWSHIP PROGRAM
> AMERICAN SOCIETY OF PLANNING OFFICIALS
> 1313 EAST 60th STREET
> CHICAGO, ILLINOIS   60637

Any American student who is a member of a minority group and who is admitted into a graduate planning program at one of the schools granted ASPO-FORD funds is eligible. For more information and a list of participating schools, write to the above address.

F-27   MINORITY FELLOWSHIPS AND ASSISTANTSHIPS IN ENVIRONMENTAL
       AND URBAN SYSTEMS

> DIVISION OF ENVIRONMENTAL AND URBAN SYSTEMS
> 201 ELIS BUILDING
> VIRGINIA POLYTECHNIC INSTITUTE AND STATE UNIVERSITY
> BLACKSBURG, VIRGINIA   24061

Graduate assistantships and Housing and Urban Development Work-Study Fellowships are offered to minority students in various graduate curricula in the Division of Environmental and Urban Systems. The graduate assistantships carry stipends up to $355 per month during the academic year (requiring 20 hours of work per week) while the work-study fellowships carry stipends of up to $3,400 per calendar year (based on the number of hours worked for government agencies during this period).

F-28   WASHINGTON JOURNALISM CENTER FELLOWSHIPS

          THE WASHINGTON JOURNALISM CENTER
          2401 VIRGINIA AVENUE, N.W.
          WASHINGTON, D. C.   20037

     The Center, an independent educational institution, awards a limited
number of fellowships for study in Washington to journalists who have had at
least two years of professional experience on newspapers or magazines of
general circulation, on wire services or in radio or television news
departments. The Fellowships run from mid-January to mid-June. The stipend
is $4,200. There are no tuition charges.

F-29   UNIVERSITY FELLOWSHIPS FOR BLACK STUDENTS AT WASHINGTON UNIVERSITY

          DEAN
          GRADUATE SCHOOL OF ARTS AND SCIENCES
          WASHINGTON UNIVERSITY
          BOX 1187
          ST. LOUIS, MISSOURI   63130

     Ten or more university fellowships for black students seeking to
begin or continue graduate study leading to the Ph.D. provide a waiver of
tuition plus $2,000 to $2,500 for the academic year.

F-30   NATIONAL CONFERENCE OF BLACK POLITICAL SCIENTISTS GRADUATE
          ASSISTANTSHIPS

          NCOBPS GRADUATE ASSISTANTSHIPS
          c/o SCHOOL OF BUSINESS AND PUBLIC ADMINISTRATION
          HOWARD UNIVERSITY
          2345 SHERMAN AVENUE, N.W.
          WASHINGTON, D. C.   20001

     A very limited number of assistantships are awarded to black
political science students beginning graduate study. Assistantships are
valued at $1,500 and students are free to attend the university of their
choice.

                              Typical Deadline: April 25

G Sources of Financial Aid Unrestricted as to Field of Study

Grants and publications pertaining to <u>specific</u> areas of study are described in the appropriate areas in preceding sections.

However, there are many programs or publications which are applicable to <u>several</u> fields of study, and these are outlined below.

All applicants for financial aid are encouraged to read this section with particular reference to the National Direct Student Loan Program, the College Work-Study Program and the Federally-Insured Student Loan Program (or such successor programs that the Congress may implement). The most important reference for current information about Federal aid is the <u>Catalog of Federal Domestic Assistance</u>. (G-25)

G-1   <u>ANNUAL REGISTER OF GRANT SUPPORT</u>

         ACADEMIC MEDIA
         14852 VENTURA BOULEVARD
         SHERMAN OAKS, CALIFORNIA   91403

         The Register is a comprehensive annual directory of fellowships and grant support programs of government agencies, foundations, business and professional organizations. It is indexed by subject, geographic area, organization and personnel. Details are given for each of over 1500 entries and include such information as type of grant; name, address and telephone number of the grant-making organization; name of grant; purpose and eligibility requirements; financial data; amount of award;and application procedures. The current edition costs $39.50.

G-2   NEED A LIFT? TO EDUCATIONAL OPPORTUNITIES, CAREERS, LOANS,
        SCHOLARSHIPS

        THE AMERICAN LEGION EDUCATIONAL AND SCHOLARSHIP PROGRAM
        DEPT. S
        P.O. BOX 1055
        INDIANAPOLIS, INDIANA   46206

        This publication revised each Fall lists sources of scholarship and
other financial aid to students, state educational benefits, some American
Legion educational aids and sources of educational assistance for veterans
and their dependents. Copies are available at 50¢ each (prepaid) or in
quantities of 100 or more at 30¢ each (prepaid) from the above address.

G-3   SCHOLARSHIPS, FELLOWSHIPS AND LOANS

        BELLMAN PUBLISHING COMPANY
        P.O. BOX 164
        ARLINGTON, MASSACHUSETTS   02174

        One of the first publications to describe a multiplicity of
financial aids, Volume V is now available at a cost of $17.00. The
publisher also offers an annual updating service, Scholarships, Fellowships
and Loans News Service, which is currently available at $20.00 per year.

G-4   STUDENT AID ANNUAL

        CHRONICLE GUIDANCE PUBLICATIONS INCORPORATED
        MORAVIA, NEW YORK   13118

        The Student Aid Annual is published yearly and contains information
on financial aid programs offered nationally or regionally by approximately
500 private and public organizations. The scope of these financial
assistance programs extends from the incoming freshman through the post-
doctoral levels. The programs include prizes, essay awards, loans, scholarships and grants. The cost is $7.50. Companion publications are Student
Aid Bulletin (States) and Student Aid Bulletin (Labor Unions) at a cost of
two dollars each.

G-5   NATURAL TRADE AND PROFESSIONAL ASSOCIATIONS OF THE UNITED
        STATES AND LABOR UNIONS

        COLUMBIA BOOKS INCORPORATED PUBLISHERS
        SUITE 601
        734 15th STREET, N.W.
        WASHINGTON, D. C.   20005

        Revised annually and available in a soft cover edition, this useful
publication lists 4700 national trade, professional and labor associations
and includes the title, address, chief officer, number of members, budget,
publications and annual meeting date. An excellent "Key Word" index
identifies organizations by field of interest, product or profession, while
a geographic index locates organizations by city and state. A budget index
and executive officer index are also provided. The publication's use in
financial aids would be for the student who has a specialized interest and
needs the names and addresses of relevant associations for direct contact as
to career opportunities or financial aids offered.

G-6   HIGHER EDUCATION SCHOLARSHIPS, STATE OF DELAWARE

        SCHOLARSHIP ADVISORY COUNCIL
        c/o STATE DEPARTMENT OF PUBLIC INSTRUCTION
        DOVER, DELAWARE

        Representative of one type of financial aid awarded residents by
various states is this program operational in the State of Delaware to grant
scholarships for professional study not available within state-supported
institutions. Such programs include architecture, forestry, dentistry, law,
medicine, optometry, pharmacy, chiropractic, social work and veterinary
medicine. Residency, need and merit are factors in awarding these scholarships. (See State and Regional Financial Aids G-17)

G-7   GRADUATE ADMISSIONS AND FELLOWSHIP SELECTION POLICIES AND
        PROCEDURES

        THE GRADUATE RECORD EXAMINATIONS BOARD
        EDUCATIONAL TESTING SERVICE
        PRINCETON, NEW JERSEY   08540

        Of primary interest to graduate school administrators and others
responsible for admission to, and aid for graduate study, this report was
written by Richard L. Burns and is based on a questionnaire sent to members
of the Council of Graduate Schools in the United States. The report
discusses the sample used and the schools' admissions policies, procedures
and criteria as well as fellowship selection policies, procedures and
criteria. In addition to statistics, current and future problems are
identified. Should also be useful to college faculty and counselors who
have advising responsibilities to seniors.

        GRADUATE PROGRAMS AND ADMISSIONS MANUAL
        BOX 2501
        PRINCETON, NEW JERSEY   08540

        Jointly sponsored by the Graduate Records Examination Board and the
Council of Graduate Schools in the United States, this publication is an
important source of information for prospective graduate students. The
Manual is updated annually and contains information about graduate programs
offered, institutional size, departmental size, academic calendar and so on.
In addition, the Manual provides specific addresses at each institution for
general information, for applications and for assistantships, fellowships
and loans. The Graduate Programs and Admissions Manual consists of four
separate volumes divided according to disciplines. The volumes are usually
available at college and university libraries and placement offices,
however, they can be ordered individually for $3.00 each. Contact the above
address for information.

G-9   LEMBERG SCHOLARSHIP LOAN FUND (JEWISH STUDENTS ONLY)

        LEMBERG SCHOLARSHIP LOAN FUND
        838 FIFTH AVENUE
        NEW YORK, NEW YORK   10021

        Awards are for Jewish men and women in a degree program at any
college or university and for pursuit of graduate or professional studies
at Jewish theological seminaries. Loans are interest free. The amount is
dependent upon need and the availability of funds and must be repaid within
ten years after completion of studies.

G-10   LOCAL RESOURCES FOR FINANCIAL AID

        Business firms, unions, professional societies, business and trade
organizations and fraternal organizations are frequently sponsors of
scholarships, grants or loans for residents of their geographic area or
children of their members. It is not feasible to attempt to list such
sources in this volume, as the number could be many hundreds, and the
restrictions on eligibility almost equally as numerous. It would appear that
most of this aid is for undergraduate study. However, the person planning
graduate or professional study should ascertain what aid is available within
his or her geographic area. Central information sources are publications of
Chambers of Commerce or the local public school system. For candidates to
professional schools, a local member of the profession should be contacted.
This book contains an interspersed annotated bibliography of many publications in the field of financial aid, and most of them should be available in
area school, college or community libraries for further research. In
addition, there is a professional association or society for nearly every
possible field of postgraduate study. Names and addresses of such societies

may be secured from the reference section of most libraries or from a
professional person in the field. Societies and associations are sources of
both career and financial aid information. (See G-5)

G-11   LOANS AND SCHOLARSHIPS FOR NEW HAMPSHIRE STUDENTS

        STATE DEPARTMENT OF EDUCATION
        CONCORD, NEW HAMPSHIRE   03301

        Representative of similar publications available for residents of a
few other states, this booklet is available to state residents without
charge. It describes loans and scholarships for which all New Hampshire
residents may be eligible, loans and scholarships for students planning to
enter certain health careers and loans and scholarships for residents of
specific communities and school districts in New Hampshire. There is also a
reference to the Citizen's Scholarship Foundation of New Hampshire, which has
grown nationally as the Dollars for Scholars program. (See State and
Regional Financial Aids G-17)

G-12   NEW YORK STATE REGENTS SCHOLAR INCENTIVE ASSISTANCE AWARDS

        REGENTS EXAMINATION AND SCHOLARSHIP CENTER
        THE STATE EDUCATION DEPARTMENT
        99 WASHINGTON AVENUE
        ALBANY, NEW YORK   12210

        The awards are made to all eligible applicants for full-time
matriculated study in an approved program of graduate or professional study
in a college in New York State. Awards vary from $100 to $600 according
to family net taxable income and may be renewed each year up to four years.
Annual application is required. (See also G-17)

G-13   NEW YORK STATE REGENTS WAR SERVICE SCHOLARSHIPS FOR VETERANS

        REGENTS EXAMINATION AND SCHOLARSHIP CENTER
        THE STATE EDUCATION DEPARTMENT
        99 WASHINGTON AVENUE
        ALBANY, NEW YORK   12210

        Six hundred (600) scholarships will be awarded to veterans of the
Armed Forces of the United States who meet the eligibility qualifications
and who succeed in the competitive examination usually held in the summer.
Each scholarship entitles the holder to payment of up to $350 a year for
tuition for a period of four years of full-time study or five years of
continuous part-time study, graduate or undergraduate, day or evening, in
any college, university, business, professional, vocational, technical or
trade school located in New York State and licensed or approved by the
Board of Regents. Candidates must have served in regular active duty from
October 1, 1961 to March 29, 1973. They must now be a legal resident of
New York State and have been a legal resident of New York State when inducted
or entered the Armed Forces. They must have been separated from active
duty under conditions not other than honorable by the date of the examination. (See also G-17)

G-14   STATE UNIVERSITY OF NEW YORK SCHOLARSHIP FOR LOW-INCOME STUDENTS

        OFFICE OF STUDENT FINANCIAL AID
        STATE UNIVERSITY OF NEW YORK
        99 WASHINGTON AVENUE
        ALBANY, NEW YORK   12210

        Designed as a supplement to the Scholar Incentive Award Program,
State University Scholarships for graduate or professional students (who
are residents of New York State, and planning to attend a unit of the State
University of New York and whose family is in the lower income category)
may receive supplemental tuition grants. Information is available from the
office of financial aid at the state university unit the candidate plans to
attend. (See also G-17)

G-15   ANNUAL GUIDES TO GRADUATE AND UNDERGRADUATE STUDY

        PETERSON'S GUIDES INCORPORATED
        P.O. BOX 123
        PRINCETON, NEW JERSEY   08540

        Books I and III-VIII outline in detail the graduate study programs
offered in 171 academic fields by various institutions. The information is
provided by the colleges and universities themselves, thus making the guides
as authoritative as they are comprehensive. Each book has three types of
 information: a graphical summary of universities and what they offer;

directories for each academic area with specific details about programs;
full-page current program descriptions written by faculty members in each
section; a bibliography of professional organizations and publications for
each major discipline; and a full explanation of accrediting. These volumes
should be of particular assistance to those seniors and upper juniors who
are just beginning their research into future graduate study. The volumes
are usually available at college and university libraries or guidance and
placement offices.

G-16   THE GRANTS REGISTER 1973-1975, POSTGRADUATE AWARDS FOR THE ENGLISH-
          SPEAKING WORLD

          ST. MARTIN'S PRESS
          175 FIFTH AVENUE
          NEW YORK, NEW YORK   10010

     The latest edition gives up-to-date information on awards for
advanced study, creative work, special projects and training. These awards
can take the form of scholarships, fellowships, lectureships, research grants,
project grants, travel grants, exchange opportunities, vacation study awards,
prizes and honoraria. ($17.50)

G-17   STATE AND REGIONAL FINANCIAL AIDS

     Every state has state-supported colleges and universities offering
a wide spectrum of graduate and professional education. Tuition and fees
are usually much lower for residents of the state. The difference between
in-state tuition and the actual cost of graduate training amounts to a
significant subsidy to the student.

     In some states where certain types of professional training are not
available within the state, programs have been established by the various
legislative bodies to subsidize the student who must attend a distant school
for that type of educational program. Mississippi, for example, provides the
out-of-state tuition charge for any resident attending an accredited
institution in another state who is seeking a graduate or professional degree
in a field of study not available in Mississippi.

     Another example is Delaware, where the General Assembly established
Higher Education Scholarships to assist residents who must study out-of-
state in the fields of architecture, forestry, dentistry, law, medicine,
optometry, pharmacy, chiropractic, social work and veterinary medicine.
These scholarships are available on the basis of need and merit, with a
limitation of $800 a year per individual.

     In several areas of the country there are Regional Education
Programs involving several states where residents of member states may
receive preferential admission to certain specialized programs as well as
being charged only in-state tuition.

The first interstate compact for higher education, The Southern Regional Education Board at 130 Sixth Street, N.W., Atlanta, Georgia 30313, has many programs such as contracts with institutions for student quotas in medicine, veterinary medicine, dentistry, public health, special education and social work, including some tuition assistance. The SREB also promotes basic research, seeks to encourage financial support of predominately black institutions and is developing training programs for mid-level work in health fields.

A third area of special aid offered by many states is for veterans of military service or children of deceased veterans whose service was credited to the state. In some states this takes the form of a cash award, and in others there is a tuition waiver in state schools and a small yearly stipend.

Some states have special aid for programs of study where a particular need is felt. Most frequently this is in the area of the study of nursing, medicine, summer programs for teachers and in fields of special education. States also participate in the Federally insured student loan program, a major source of funds described elsewhere in this book. Only a few states (e.g., Connecticut) have special state scholarship grants for graduate students.

Information about state financial aid from any state may be secured directly and in current form from the particular state education department.

G-18   ARMY R.O.T.C.

PROFESSOR OF MILITARY SCIENCE
U. S. ARMY R.O.T.C.
BARTON HALL
CORNELL UNIVERSITY
ITHACA, NEW YORK   14850

Degree candidates who plan to enter a university for a graduate or professional program of at least two years duration may be interested in the "two-year program" option of Army R.O.T.C. The unit at Cornell University acts as the information and application center for central New York State, but universities with this program are located nationwide. The subsistence payment is $100 monthly. Scholarships are available on a competitive basis.

G-19   CUBAN EDUCATION - STUDENT LOANS

          U. S. OFFICE OF EDUCATION
          DIVISION OF STUDENT ASSISTANCE, BHE
          PROGRAM SUPPORT BRANCH
          CUBAN LOAN SECTION
          WASHINGTON, D. C.   20202

     Participating universities are authorized to loan funds to their
undergraduate or graduate students who are Cuban nationals who cannot
receive support from inside Cuba and who have demonstrated financial need.
At the graduate or professional level, up to $2,500 per year may be borrowed.
Up to ten years is allowed for repayment at low interest rates. Contact
should be the financial aid officer at the college the applicant plans to
attend.

G-20   THE COLLEGE WORK-STUDY PROGRAM

          U. S. OFFICE OF EDUCATION
          DIVISION OF STUDENT ASSISTANCE
          WASHINGTON, D. C.   20202

     The financial aid officer of each college or university is
responsible for determining the students to be employed and conditions of
employment. Students usually are employed for an average of fifteen hours
weekly during the academic year and up to forty hours weekly during summer
or vacation, depending on funds available within the institution. This
program is for students who are determined to have great need.

G-21   GUARANTEED STUDENT LOAN PROGRAM

            DIVISION OF INSURED LOANS, BHE
            OFFICE OF EDUCATION, DHEW
            WASHINGTON, D. C.   20202

      Banks, credit unions, pension funds, savings and loan associations,
etc., are eligible to become lenders under this program which is subsidized
and supervised by the Federal government Loans are approved or denied at
the discretion of the lender. For those students who demonstrate financial
need, the Federal government will pay all interest which accrues while the
student is in school. Repayment schedules are in installments over a
period of from five to ten years but may be deferred while the borrower is
a member of the Armed Forces, Peace Corps or Vista. Apply directly to
lenders. Approximately six billion dollars have been loaned to nearly
3.5 million students since the program began in 1965. Further details about
the current program may be secured from the financial aid officer of the
university the student is planning to attend.

G-22   NATIONAL DIRECT STUDENT LOAN PROGRAM

            U. S. OFFICE OF EDUCATION
            DIVISION OF STUDENT ASSISTANCE
            WASHINGTON, D. C.   20202

      This college-administered loan program makes it possible to borrow
up to $10,000 for graduate or professional study. (This total includes any
amount borrowed under NDSL for undergraduate study.) Repayment begins nine
months after the borrower ceases at least half-time study and may extend
over ten years at relatively low interest rates. No repayment is required
during periods of military service or with the Peace Corps or Vista. There
is a proportional cancellation feature for students entering teaching or the
Armed Forces. Loans are limited by the amounts available from individual
universities, family income and are determined by the financial aid officer
on the individual campus.

G-23   URBAN MASS TRANSPORTATION GRANTS

          DIRECTOR
          UNIVERSITY GRANT PROGRAMS DIVISION
          OFFICE OF RESEARCH, DEVELOPMENT AND DEMONSTRATIONS
          URBAN MASS TRANSPORTATION ADMINISTRATION
          DEPARTMENT OF TRANSPORTATION
          WASHINGTON, D. C.   20590

          Grants for research and training in urban transportation problems
are made directly to universities. Such grants are used to conduct competent and qualified research into the theoretical or practical problems of
urban transportation and to provide for the training of persons to carry on
further research or to obtain employment in private or public organizations
which plan, construct, operate or manage urban transportation systems. A
brochure listing universities with grants, the research projects and the
student stipends is available from the address above.

G-24   TAX INFORMATION FOR AMERICAN SCHOLARS IN THE U.S. AND ABROAD

          TREASURY DEPARTMENT
          INTERNAL REVENUE SERVICE

          This leaflet defines what the tax law means by such terms as
scholarship, fellowship grant, scholarship prizes and research fellowship.
There is also an explanation of tax exemption for various government grants
as well as compensation for services. Available from any IRS District
Office at no charge.

G-25   CATALOGUE OF FEDERAL DOMESTIC ASSISTANCE

          SUPERINTENDENT OF DOCUMENTS
          U. S. GOVERNMENT PRINTING OFFICE
          WASHINGTON, D. C.   20402

          This publication, prepared annually in loose-leaf form and includ-
ing updating bulletins, is available at a cost of $7.25 and includes
descriptions of all Federal domestic assistance programs. Several hundred
programs are indexed and described. The Catalogue is compiled for the
Executive Office of the President by the Office of Management and Budget.
Only a small fraction of the entries concern fellowships, traineeships,
student financial aid or scholarships. The book should be available in
municipal and university libraries. It has the additional merit of being
updated periodically so that information about all types of government
assistance programs added, altered or deleted as funding fluctuates is kept
current.

G-26   GRADUATE TEACHING ASSISTANTS IN AMERICAN UNIVERSITIES: A REVIEW
        OF RECENT TRENDS AND RECOMMENDATIONS

            SUPERINTENDENT OF DOCUMENTS
            U. S. GOVERNMENT PRINTING OFFICE
            WASHINGTON, D. C.   20402

            This 70-page report has been prepared by the Bureau of Higher
        Education of the U. S. Department of Health, Education and Welfare and is
        available for 40 cents at the address above. The publication brings
        together the results of numerous studies and papers concerning teaching
        assistants and their impact on undergraduate instructions, the effect on
        progress toward advanced degrees, their status within the academic
        hierarchy, their working hours and the percents of stipends awarded by
        field and area. (Catalog Number HE 5.258:58039; Stock No. (S/N) 1780-0692)

G-27   INVENTORY OF FEDERAL PROGRAMS INVOLVING EDUCATIONAL ACTIVITIES
        CONCERNED WITH IMPROVING INTERNATIONAL UNDERSTANDING AND
        COOPERATION

            SUPERINTENDENT OF DOCUMENTS
            U.S. GOVERNMENT PRINTING OFFICE
            WASHINGTON, D. C.   20402

            Prepared in 1969 by the U. S. Department of Health, Education and
        Welfare, Office of Education, this 545-page publication reproduces
        elements of a survey of 31 agencies reporting on 159 programs relevant to
        the title. The reports deal in depth with educational activities of AID,
        AEC, DOD, the Office of Education, The Public Health Service, the Interior
        Department, the National Academy of Sciences, National Foundation on the
        Arts and Humanities, National Science Foundation, Peace Corps, State
        Department and many lesser-known agencies and programs. (Price $4.75,
        Catalog Number HE 5.214:14142)

G-28   A SELECTED LIST OF MAJOR FELLOWSHIP OPPORTUNITIES AND AIDS TO
        ADVANCED EDUCATION FOR UNITED STATES CITIZENS

            FELLOWSHIP OFFICE
            NATIONAL ACADEMY OF SCIENCES
            2101 CONSTITUTION AVENUE, N.W.
            WASHINGTON, D. C.   20418

            This pamphlet was prepared by the Fellowship Office, Office of
        Scientific Personnel, National Research Council, on contract with the
        National Science Foundation and is available free upon request. There is
        a short section on undergraduate aid as well as brief descriptions of suppo
        for graduate and professional study and postdoctoral awards.

G-29   <u>OCCUPATIONAL OUTLOOK HANDBOOK</u>

SUPERINTENDENT OF DOCUMENTS
U. S. GOVERNMENT PRINTING OFFICE
WASHINGTON, D. C.   20402

Revised annually by the Bureau of Labor Statistics of the United
States Department of Labor, this is a most authoritative source of career
information which includes descriptions of professional opportunities,
typical educational requirements, a statement on financial aid, earning
trends, employment outlook, etc. Current editions are usually available
in libraries and educational guidance and placement offices.

G-30   NATIONAL ENDOWMENT FOR THE HUMANITIES

DIRECTOR, DIVISION OF FELLOWSHIPS
NATIONAL ENDOWMENT FOR THE HUMANITIES
806 15th STREET, N.W.
WASHINGTON, D. C.   20506

The purpose of the National Endowment for the Humanities fellowships is to help humanists develop their abilities as teachers, scholars
and interpreters of the humanities. The Endowment offers various fellowship programs for persons at different stages in their careers, at
different types of institutions and with different projects. The programs
vary in length from summer support to academic-year awards. Although
applicants need not have advanced degrees, degree candidates are not
eligible, nor may work done under a fellowship be applied toward a degree.
General information and application materials are available from the
Division of Fellowships.

G-31   <u>SUMMARY OF EDUCATIONAL ASSISTANCE BENEFITS FOR VETERANS WITH
SERVICE SINCE JANUARY 31, 1955</u>

VETERANS ADMINISTRATION
WASHINGTON, D. C.   20402

The Veterans Administration offers financial assistance for eligible
veterans enrolled in a full or part-time course of study in an approved
educational institution. Most veterans with service after January 31, 1955
are eligible for these benefits; however, the V.A. decides eligibility on
each application. Currently, a single student who is enrolled full-time may
receive $220 per month; with one dependent he may receive $261 per month.
Eligibility ceases eight years from the date of release from service after
January 31, 1955 or May 31, 1974, whichever is later. For additional
information, write to the V.A. regional office in your state.

G-32   EDUCATIONAL ASSISTANCE FOR SONS AND DAUGHTERS, WIVES AND WIDOWS OF
        DECEASED OR TOTALLY DISABLED VETERANS

        VETERANS ADMINISTRATION
        DEPARTMENT OF VETERANS BENEFITS
        WASHINGTON, D. C.   20420

        This V.A. pamphlet 22-73-3, revised in June of 1973, outlines
eligibility, benefits and application procedure for children, wives and
widows of deceased or disabled veterans who wish to continue their education
full or part-time in technical schools, colleges, universities or on-the-job
training. In addition to the basic monthly allowance (currently $220 per
month for up to 36 months), handicapped children may receive special
assistance.

G-33   THE UNIVERSITY AS A SOURCE OF FINANCIAL AID

        Most universities publish booklets on financial aid available
through the university, listing all resources internal and external. Some
large graduate departments have also published booklets describing their
particular admissions procedures and policies and describing specialized
programs and the types of financial aid available in each specialization, as
well as those available in all disciplines.

        Typical examples are: Financial Aid for Graduate Students from the
Graduate School and the Office of Student Financial Aids, The University of
Wisconsin, Madison and Graduate Programs in Psychology, Department of
Psychology, University of Minnesota, Minneapolis 55455.

        It is most important that the candidate obtain information about
admission and financial aid from each department or school to which he might
apply about one year in advance of the date of probable attendance.

        The current trend is for both foundations and the Federal government
to reduce the number of fellowships available upon direct application, and
they are instead making grants to universities for research projects which
provide financial aid to the graduate student in the form of traineeships
and research assistantships.

Additional Bibliography

American College Testing Program. <u>Financing Higher Education:
Alternatives for the Federal Government</u>. P.O. Box 168, Iowa City,
Iowa 52240: M. D. Orwig, Editor, 1971. (This is a 390-page book contain-
ing a series of position papers on various ways of funding higher education.
The papers deal with economic issues, social issues and the question of who
should pay the mounting costs of higher education.)

<u>The Foundation Directory</u>, Edition 4, prepared by the Foundation
Center, and available for Fall 1971 distribution through Columbia University
Press, 136 South Broadway, Irvington, New York 10533, at a cost of fifteen
dollars. This revision includes valuable data on 5,300 foundations, each of
which has assets in excess of $500,000 or which made grants of $25,000 or
more in the year of record. One index is by field of interest.

Index

DATE DUE

Demco, Inc. 38-293